POWER TO THE PARASITES!

POWER TO THE PARASITES!

CHELSEA L. WOOD
ILLUSTRATED BY DAVE MOTTRAM

GODWIN BOOKS
HENRY HOLT AND COMPANY
NEW YORK

Henry Holt and Company, *Publishers since 1866*
Henry Holt® is a registered trademark of Macmillan Publishing Group, LLC
120 Broadway, New York, NY 10271 • mackids.com

Our books may be purchased in bulk for promotional, educational, or
business use. Please contact your local bookseller or the Macmillan Corporate
and Premium Sales Department at (800) 221-7945 ext. 5442 or by email at
MacmillanSpecialMarkets@macmillan.com.

Library of Congress Control Number: 2023045560

First edition, 2024
Book design by Meg Sayre
Printed in the United States of America by BVG, Fairfield, Pennsylvania

ISBN 978-1-250-83398-3
1 3 5 7 9 10 8 6 4 2

TO ARMAND KURIS, KEVIN LAFFERTY, AND
RYAN HECHINGER, WHO FIRST SHOWED ME THE
DOOR TO THE SECRET TREASURE ROOM.

AND TO KEN FERGUSON, WHO HELPED ME OPEN IT.

CONTENTS

Note: Words that are in **bold** are included in the glossary at the end of the book.

INTRODUCTION

~ 1 ~

THE SECRET

I wasn't always interested in parasites. When I was in the seventh grade, one of my teachers gave our class an assignment: write and draw about what your life would be like in ten years. That assignment was easy for me because my mind was already made up. I had decided that I would be a marine biologist, and that I would study whales and dolphins. What I didn't know at the time was that the *really* interesting **organisms** were not the whales and dolphins themselves. The tiny creatures living *inside* whales and dolphins are far more fascinating, beautiful, and awe-inspiring. These creatures—called

parasites—are the stars of this book. We call the parasites' victims **hosts**, and we define a parasite as any organism that lives inside or on a host and causes harm to that host.

In ten years, I picture myself working for a doctorate in marine biology at Stoney brook University. I will probably be planning to work at an aquarium, and then maybe work up to having my own reasearch boat, and studying sea mammals—probably dolphins or whales.

Chelsea Wood

Actual assignment completed by the author
when she was in seventh grade

I wrote this book to let you in on a secret: Parasites are all around you, all the time, hidden in plain sight. To find a mysterious world that most people don't even know is there, you don't need to look any farther than your mom, your dog, the squirrel that hangs out in your backyard, your best friend, that lion you saw in a nature video once, and—yes—even yourself. This hidden world includes the worms hanging out in your intestine, the tiny ticks that skitter across your skin in summertime, and the head lice that force your parents to keep you home from school. Parasites draw energy from their hosts in a variety of sneaky ways, including bloodsucking, food-stealing, and organ-eating. They are tiny and tucked inside their hosts, so they mostly escape notice. Honestly, parasites probably remain mysterious and unknown in part because it makes us all feel better not to think about them. What kind of person wants to think about the worms and bugs living inside their own bodies? Well, me, for one. And hopefully by the end of this book, you'll also be interested in peeking below the surface of the everyday world to catch a glimpse of the secret world of parasites!

I think it is worth paying attention to parasites for a few reasons. First, parasites are jaw-droppingly, ridiculously, mind-bendingly weird. Truly, working as a **parasitologist** is like getting to watch nonstop horror movies back-to-back for your entire career. Yes, it can be scary—but the job has never, for a single second, left me bored. In fact, science fiction books and movies frequently draw ideas directly from the world of actual, real-life parasites (as you will see in chapter 7).

But beyond being endlessly, horrifically fascinating, it turns out parasites are also pretty important. You would never guess it, considering that they are rarely mentioned in school. I never heard even a peep about parasites from my teachers until I was in college! But even though most middle school and even high school teachers are perfectly happy to skip right over the parasites and their flesh-gnawing, bloodsucking, poop-inhabiting lifestyles, parasites pretty much run the world. Parasites help to reduce the number of their hosts, preventing Earth from being overrun by, say, insects (chapter 7) or rats (chapter 16). Parasites help deliver food to animals who need it (chapter 10). They might even help us fight human **diseases** (chapter 17).

Learning about the secret world of parasites turned my life upside down, leading me along a path that I would never have imagined for myself when I was sitting in my seventh-grade classroom. But among the most surprising twists in the tale of my scientific life is this one: I never thought that slimy, squirmy, poop-flecked parasites would lead me to—of all things—love.

~ 2 ~

HOW I LEARNED TO LOVE EARTH'S MOST UNLOVABLE CREATURES

You've already heard a little bit from me, but we haven't yet been formally introduced. Hi, I'm Chelsea. I'm a professor of ecology at a university, which means that I'm a scientist who studies the environment. I do scientific research on **parasites**, and I teach my students about them.

In seventh grade, I predicted that I would become a marine biologist. That prediction came true in some ways but not in others. I sometimes do scientific research projects in the ocean, which technically makes me a marine biologist. But most marine biologists study fish, snails, **plankton**, or dolphins, while I study the parasites *inside* those **organisms**. The other thing that makes my research unique is that I occasionally do projects on parasites that live in rivers or ponds, or on land. So I'm really more of a parasite ecologist than a marine biologist.

"But wait," you ask, "how did your life run so badly off the rails? You were on track to swim with dolphins, and now you sift through poop to find worms. What went wrong?"

Well, like a lot of tales of people who cross over to the dark side, this one begins with a love story.

I was in graduate school and working toward a doctoral degree in ecology when our eyes first met. His were big and brown, drawn open wide as if terrified, welled up with tears. A fringe of white fanned out from his lash line like fake eyelashes that were just a bit too dramatic. As I looked him in the eye for the very first time, I couldn't help myself. I fell head over heels. The love of my scientific life is shown on page 10.

No, I am not in love with a wild cow. Not literally anyway and not with the cow, but with its lovely false eyelashes. All it took was that one look to turn me away from whale-watching for the rest of my life. These parasitic moths are so specialized that the only meals they eat in their whole lives are the tears of an endangered cow in the remotest forests of Southeast Asia. Seeing this species for the first time made me realize: There is so much weirdness to discover in the world! Parasites have invented some astonishing ways to survive, lifestyles that are strange and unfamiliar to us, that are dazzling in their uniqueness. I was hooked.

My love of parasites has taken me on adventures all over the world. I've gone scuba diving on the world's most beautiful coral reefs, where I trapped a bunch of colorful fishes and examined them for parasites. I've mucked around in the rivers of Senegal in West Africa, where I sifted through mud to find the tiny snails that

Lachryphagous (tear-drinking) moths feeding on the tears of a banteng (an endangered species of wild cow) in Southeast Asia

transmit a terrible parasitic worm to the people who live there. I've traveled around Bangladesh in South Asia, tracking a virus that bats spread to people. I have followed where the parasites lead, and since parasites do not care about national borders, I've gotten to hop, skip, and jump across Earth. This book is my chance to share these parasitological adventures with you.

I was not interested in parasites when I first learned about them in a college class. I thought that they were slimy, icky, and too small to be interesting. I thought that they were jerks for stealing their dinner while their hardworking **hosts** did all the hunting, gathering, eating, and digesting for them. I thought that they were unimportant and that the world would be better off without them. It was only when I finally came face-to-face with living parasites that I realized how spectacularly beautiful many of them are. I was awestruck by the wild stunts they pull to stay alive and the vital roles they play in keeping **ecosystems** healthy. Yes, they are *bad* for their hosts; but they are often *good* for the ecosystems in which they occur. It might feel odd to think of parasites as *good guys*—but they really, truly are. I hope that this book convinces you. And maybe—just maybe—you will fall in love with parasites, too.

STUFF YOU NEED TO KNOW BEFORE WE GET STARTED

You are entering a dimension that you've probably never even peeked into before: **parasite** world. So before we leap in, let's get a couple of things straight.

PARASITES OFTEN LOOK SUPER-DUPER OUTLANDISH.

A fish is a fish is a fish: Even though they differ in color, size, and shape, there isn't a fish on this planet that you would mistake for, say, a bird. How boring! Parasites would never be so unimaginative. They come in a baffling array of shapes. Some will look just like the roots of a tree or the filaments of a fungus—even though they are indeed animals. Brace yourself: Many parasites look like worms or fleas just like you'd expect, but others take on fantastical body shapes.

WHAT IS A PARASITE AND WHAT IS NOT?

As we learned in chapter 1, parasites are organisms that live inside or on other organisms, causing harm in the process. We call the parasites' victims **hosts**. Any organism that does not live inside or on another organism is **free-living**.

REPRODUCTION IS THE NAME OF THE GAME.

Out in nature, **organisms** (including parasites) are after only one thing: reproduction. This is because all organisms have been shaped by evolution. Organisms that don't reproduce leave no offspring behind when they die. Organisms that reproduce a lot leave many offspring, and their offspring have many offspring. As a result, the only organisms that persist in nature are the ones that are very good at reproducing. That is why you'll notice throughout the book that parasites are always trying to either reproduce (so they leave behind lots of offspring) or eat (so they can stay alive long enough to reproduce). It might seem a little silly to be so single-minded, but nature is brutal and the parasites that exist today are here because their ancestors found tried-and-true ways to reproduce.

For parasites, reproduction can happen in one of two ways: sexually or asexually. Sexual reproduction occurs when parasites mate with each other and combine their **genes** to create babies. This is awesome, because when genes from two different parents mix together, they result in babies who differ from one another— just as human siblings differ from one another. But parasites are also capable of asexual repro- duction, which is a neat trick that not every ani- mal species can do. Asexual reproduction can be accomplished in a variety of ways, but the simplest way is for a mom to just have babies without mating first. Her babies will be exact replicas of her—just as if you had an identical twin and both of you were identical to your mom! Asexual reproduction lets parasites pump out lots of babies, but because they are all identical, they are a risky investment. Having many of the exact same kind of offspring means that they are all equally vulnerable to changes in the environment. Having lots of different kinds of offspring means that at least one offspring will have the combination of genes it needs to handle changes in the environment, survive, and reproduce itself. So while asexual reproduction is great and all, the crowning achievement of a parasite's life is sexual reproduction. And they will go to great lengths to get there.

MANY PARASITES HAVE RIDICULOUSLY COMPLICATED LIFE CYCLES.

You know how caterpillars will spin cocoons and later emerge as butterflies? In this process, a baby caterpillar completely transforms the appearance of its body and becomes an adult butterfly. Parasites also have life cycles where a single individual transitions through very different-looking stages—parasites just make it way, way more complicated than any caterpillar can manage.

Parasites with **complex life cycles** require at least two different host species to complete their development. A good example comes from a group of worms called the trematodes. Trematodes begin their lives in the gut of **vertebrates**—like birds, mammals, reptiles, or fish—which we call the **definitive hosts** because they are the hosts in which sexual reproduction takes place. There, the **adult** trematode settles down with a mate and produces **eggs**, which are pooped out by the host into the environment. The eggs hatch and go on to infect a snail, which we call the **first intermediate host**—"intermediate" because it is the host of a larval stage of the parasite, and "first" because it is host to the first larval stage after hatching. Within the snail, the **larvae**

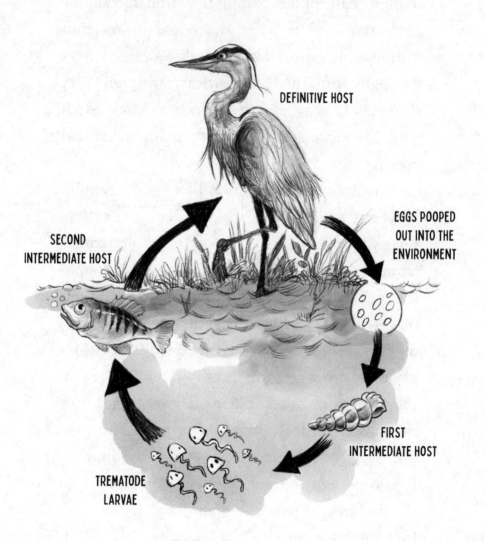

DEFINITIVE HOST

EGGS POOPED
OUT INTO THE
ENVIRONMENT

SECOND
INTERMEDIATE HOST

FIRST
INTERMEDIATE HOST

TREMATODE
LARVAE

Complex life cycle of a trematode

clone themselves asexually, sending thousands of those clones out into the water in search of a **second intermediate host**. When they find that second intermediate host—perhaps a small fish—the parasite creates a **cyst** in that host's body, where it lays in wait. When the second intermediate host is consumed by a definitive host, the life cycle is complete. I told you it was complicated!

I want you to be prepared: Many parasites do this hopscotching, moving from one host to another just to complete one turn of their life cycle. It's like taking a highway to get to your next-door neighbor's house. Parasites love to make life complicated.

Okay, now that we've covered the basics, let's get started!

PART I

PARASITES DOING STUFF
OUT IN NATURE

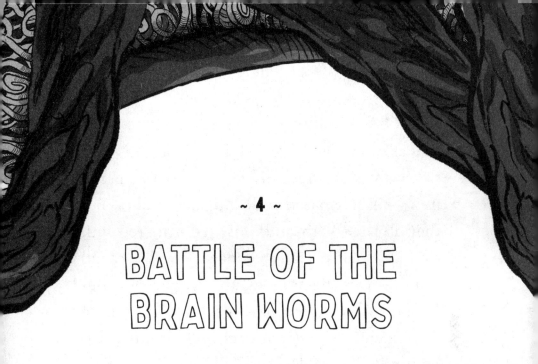

~ 4 ~

BATTLE OF THE BRAIN WORMS

If you've ever watched a nature documentary, you know that the animal world can be brutal. In 1850, the British poet Alfred Tennyson wrote of "Nature, red in tooth and claw"; I think what Tennyson meant is that, although a sunny day on the African savanna might seem at first like a delight, it'll be substantially less delightful when a lion is feasting on your carcass. But you don't have to travel all the way to the savanna to see nature's spectacular brutality up close.

Not far from where I grew up in New York,

scenes of similar callous violence play out every day, only a bit more hidden from view than a lion's kill. Nematodes do not have claws, but they do have teeth, and those teeth are red with the blood of many familiar mammals. Also called roundworms, nematodes are everywhere. But I want to talk about one species of nematode in particular: *Parelaphostrongylus tenuis* (pronounced: PAR-eh-laff-oh-STRON-jill-us- TEN-you-iss). Because that scientific name is kind of a mouthful, we'll simply call this dude "brain worm."

The name might give away this little worm's game: Its favorite place to be is in the brain of deer, especially white-tailed deer, which are common across North America. But the worm has a **complex life cycle**, which introduces a challenge: How does the **parasite** get from one **host** deer to the next?

The brain worm has solved this problem like an evil genius would. Snails host the larval stages of the parasite. When deer munch on greenery, they sometimes accidentally chow down on an infected snail. Yippee for the parasite! It can now bust out of the intestinal tract

The brain worm (Parelaphostrongylus tenuis)
with its intermediate host (snail) and definitive
host (white-tailed deer)

of the deer, follow the spinal nerves up to the spine, follow the spine up to the brain, and settle into its comfy new home in the deer's skull. By now, the worm has matured into an **adult**, and it can pair up with a mate to produce **eggs**. The parents almost immediately say goodbye to these eggs, which—even though they have only just been born—now embark on a long solo migration. Departing their childhood home in the brain, the eggs are deposited into the bloodstream and ride that gushing water park ride straight to the lungs. There, they hatch into **larvae** and crawl up the tube that connects the lungs to the throat and down the tube that connects the throat to the stomach. Once in the intestine, they can be pooped out into the world—hopefully near some nice juicy snails. And with that, the circle of brain worm life is complete!

Of course, when worms take up residence in the brain of a deer, it isn't great news for the deer. Once a brain worm makes a comfy home for itself inside the deer's skull, it can stick around for the rest of the deer's life. Unless a very large number of worms are attempting to share the limited space inside one skull, the parasites steer clear of the deer's brain, preferring instead to nestle into the feathery soft tissues that surround the brain—just the same way that you might snuggle into some soft blankets on the couch, rather than tearing open the couch cushions and wedging yourself inside of them. This means that infected deer might be a smidge slower to react or a bit clumsier than normal, but these are generally the worst signs of infection for white-tailed deer. All in all, pretty lucky, considering that they have worms in their brains.

Unfortunately, brain worms aren't quite so kind to other host species. White-tailed deer are the preferred hosts of this parasite, meaning that our brain worm finds it nice and easy to settle down in the skulls of white-tailed deer and start a family. Other hosts don't offer the kind of skull habitat that this parasite needs to thrive, so when a brain worm accidentally finds itself in this unsuitable habitat, it throws an epic tantrum, tearing open the couch cushions

Moose showing signs of brain worm infection

in the process. When moose, elk, caribou, reindeer (sorry, Santa!), mule deer, sheep, goats, or alpacas accidentally eat a brain worm–infested snail, it's sort of like they've just invited an angry bull to come inside and browse the delicate items in their china shop. Out of spite, the worm burrows into the spine and sometimes the brain; you probably won't be surprised to learn that having your brain drilled by a worm can result in some bizarre behaviors.

Any host other than white-tailed deer will tend to have major **neurological** problems in response to a brain worm infection. It might start with a bit of clumsiness; perhaps our infected moose is a little slower to react to a threat than it used to be, taking a few extra seconds to flee when it happens upon a predator. But soon, more noticeable symptoms appear. The moose might hold its head in an unusual position; it might start pacing in circles; it might lose its fear of humans, stumbling among houses and busy streets that it would normally avoid; it might stop feeding and waste away. Many infected moose ultimately die. Maybe it should be "Nature, pink in tooth and claw," since these parasites have not blood but brains on their metaphorical hands.

Because brain worm is such a deadly infection for moose but a relatively benign one for white-tailed deer, the parasite has become something of an ally to white-tailed deer in their never-ending competition with moose for food and habitat. Both white-tailed deer and moose live in some of the same northern states of the United States and the southern provinces of Canada. White-tailed deer can't survive cold weather the way that moose can, so they leave the moose to the chillier, more northerly habitats. But as climate change causes the weather to warm, white-tailed deer are moving north, and they are bringing brain worm with them. This is because, anywhere there are white-tailed deer, there will be white-tailed deer poop. And anywhere this poop occurs, there can be snails infected with brain worm. As brain worm follows white-tailed deer north, the threat of this parasite is chasing moose into ever-more-northerly habitats—all thanks to the one-two punch of climate change and brain worm.

Luckily for us, this particular brain worm has never been reported to infect people. That's probably due to two things: first, the parasite is adapted only to live in some hoofed mammals and, second, humans rarely eat live snails. In fact, only a tiny fraction of all parasites on Earth infect people. Don't get me wrong—there are still plenty of human-infecting parasites, and we'll talk about some of them in later chapters. But there are thousands upon thousands of parasites that infect wildlife, which means that the brain worm is far from unique. In fact, it isn't even the only wildlife parasite that can make its host wander in circles until it dies.

~ 5 ~

'ROUND AND 'ROUND WE GO! AND WHERE DO WE STOP? DEATH!

Maybe that last chapter shook you up a bit. I mean, moose are such majestic creatures, symbolic of pristine wilderness—who wants to imagine that their brains are being turned into Swiss cheese by burrowing worms? Maybe you're hugging yourself and rocking in a corner and repeating, "It's just moose; it's just moose; it's just moose." If so, I'm sorry to burst your bubble. It's not just moose. **Parasites** are every-where, all the time. Maybe, if you're like me, the

A jellyfish alongside its tiny, long-lost cousin:
the whirling disease parasite
Myxobolus cerebralis

thought of this alternate dimension of life—this secret world full of parasites that act like puppet masters pulling the strings behind the scenes—fills you with excitement. If so, you're going to love this next parasite.

The whirling disease parasite, *Myxobolus cerebralis* (pronounced mix-AH-bull-iss ser-ee-BRA-liss), is not an impressive specimen. This tiny guy is just a few **cells** stuck together, invisible to the naked eye. It can be found infecting freshwater fish, specifically salmon and trout, in the rivers, streams, and lakes of Europe, Russia, North America, South Africa, New Zealand, and a few countries in South America. For a long time, scientists thought that the whirling disease parasite was related to the simple, single-celled parasite that causes **malaria** in people. Those scientists could not have been more wrong because, as it turns out, this minuscule parasite that lives exclusively in freshwater habitats, infecting freshwater fish, is actually related to jellyfish. That is not a typo. Millions of years ago, the whirling disease parasite's ancestor was pulsating through the ocean, waving its stinging tentacles. Slowly, evolution shaped it from a large animal that lives in the ocean to a small animal that lives inside freshwater fish. The fact that parasitic shrunken jellyfishes are a thing is proof that truth is stranger than fiction; nature is so much more odd than anything the human imagination can dream up.

Now, let's make things even weirder by talking about how this tiny jellyfish makes its parasitic living. Remember how last chapter's brain worm had a **complex life cycle**, where it used more than one **host** species, with larval stages of the parasite living in one host species and adult stages of the parasite living in a completely different host species? Well, the whirling disease parasite has a complex life cycle of its own. **Adult parasites** live inside worm hosts (technically speaking, *Tubifex tubifex*, pronounced TUBE-if-ex TUBE-if-ex) burrowed into the sediment of rivers, streams, and lakes. These hosts resemble earthworms, but unlike earthworms they live only underwater. Inside the worm host's intestinal tract,

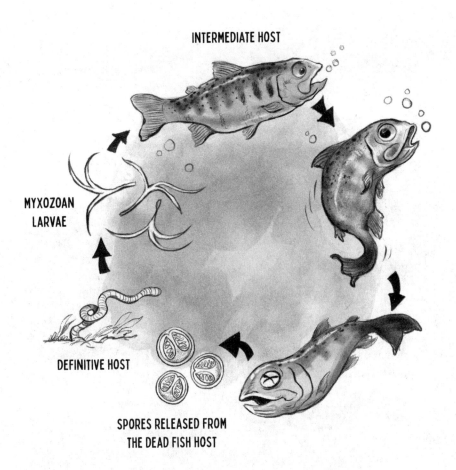

Life cycle of Myxobolus cerebralis

Trout with whirling disease

the whirling disease parasite reproduces; its babies are released into the water when the worm poops. At this stage, as the parasite's babies go out in search of a fish host, they look kind of like . . . jeez, I don't know. A three-pronged fishing hook? They certainly don't look anything like their jellyfish selves. As soon as this fishing-hook stage intersects with the skin of a salmon or trout, the parasite injects itself into the host's body and heads for the skeleton. There it replicates itself some more through asexual reproduction, damaging the fish so badly that the host dies, decomposes, and releases all the parasitic clones to find a new worm host and start the life cycle all over again.

Okay, let's get to the name. Why do I persist in calling our tiny, adorable parasitic jellyfish the "whirling disease parasite"? Well, the **disease** that this parasite causes in fish, whirling disease, was named because of the behavior of infected fish. Once inside the skeleton of its salmon or trout host, the parasite eats the fish's bones. This, as you can imagine, is not awesome for the fish. Damage to the spinal cord and brain can bend the fish's body in such a way that it is constantly chasing its tail fin instead of swimming forward. Some infected fish can swim forward but do so only in a whirling, corkscrew motion instead of their normal, straight-line motion. Infected fish are sometimes so damaged that they are unable to feed or avoid predators. You might think to yourself: Why would a parasite want to cause such life-threatening symptoms in its host when the parasite's life depends on the host continuing to live? The answer is simple: The parasite causes these serious symptoms only when it is ready to move on to the next stage in its life cycle. The death of the fish suits the whirling disease parasite just fine, because the parasite will emerge from the fish's carcass and move on, without a thought, to its next host.

The whirling disease parasite is native to Europe—that is, it evolved in Europe and Europe is where it is supposed to be. But this lucky parasite infects salmon and trout, which humans love to eat. To satisfy our appetite for fish, we've shipped living European salmon and trout all over the world, and the whirling disease parasite has used that opportunity to hitch rides to North America, South Africa, New Zealand, and South America. The parasite is non-native in these regions, which is a problem. Non-native parasites are often very dangerous, because native hosts (like native salmon and trout species) have never encountered them before and have few defenses against them. Such is the case with whirling disease in North America; outbreaks of this parasite damage native salmon and trout populations, which are already suffering from the presence of dams, pollution, and fishing pressure.

The whirling disease parasite is a great example of a species that is thriving as humans increasingly mess up **ecosystems**; it now infects fish all around the world—a major achievement for a parasite that used to be relegated to a single continent. But not all parasites are able to take advantage of human interference in the environment. In fact, some parasites are following their endangered hosts straight to extinction.

~ 6 ~

WHAT LOUSY LUCK

After reading the last two chapters, you might be thinking to yourself, "The **parasites** are taking over, run for the hills!" Maybe you're already building your anti-parasite bunker, surrounded by cans of insecticide, boiling your water before you drink it, murmuring about the parasite apocalypse. After all, you just read about a brain-boring worm that is expanding northward due to climate change and a bone-melting jellyfish that has hitchhiked around the world. But, as it turns out, parasites have as much to fear from us as we do from them. Although the nasty things we humans do to **ecosystems** (like global warming and pollution) can cause some parasites to increase, we're driving just as many parasites—and maybe more—to the brink of extinction and beyond.

Consider the California condor louse (*Colpocephalum californici*, pronounced cole-poh-SEF-ah-lum cal-i-FORN-ee-chee). The **host** of this very special louse—the California condor—has never won a beauty contest, but it is a species that is much-beloved among Californians. After all, its bald, wrinkly head is kind of endearing, and its **wingspan** is nearly ten feet, making it a pretty impressive flier. Like all good members of the vulture family, the California condor feeds on dead things. But despite its lack of conventional beauty and decent table manners, Californians have rallied behind the condor—in part because it very nearly went extinct.

California condors used to be abundant across the US West Coast and Southwest, at one point ranging as far north as Washington State. But by 1987, the once-massive population (estimated to be fifty thousand individuals at its peak) had been reduced to only twenty-two birds. There were lots of reasons for this nosedive in the condors' abundance. Because they have the habit of feeding on dead animals, condors often pick at carcasses left behind by hunters; these carcasses contain the lead bullets that had turned the animal into a carcass in the first place. Lead is a potent poison for any living thing but especially condors, whose strong digestive juices break down the bullets and increase the bird's absorption of toxic lead. To make matters worse, condors can be the target of poachers and egg collectors, are sensitive to the insecticide DDT, often fly into power lines and die of electrocution, and have had much of their native habitat turned into suburbs and shopping malls. No wonder they were on a fast track to extinction!

In the 1980s, conservation groups launched a last-ditch effort to rescue the California condor from oblivion. The last remaining twenty-two birds were brought into captivity at the San Diego Wild Animal Park (now called the San

Diego Zoo Safari Park) and the Los Angeles Zoo. Before anything else was done to nurture these few remaining representatives of the species, conservationists took a sensible precautionary measure: They treated each bird with a powdered chemical to kill any parasites that might be living in its feathers. After all, they didn't want biting, chewing, bloodsucking lice, mites, fleas, or ticks to endanger the recovery of these precious few condors. And with this simple delousing, well-intentioned conservationists working *against* extinction very nearly *caused* an extinction: that of the California condor louse.

It wasn't the conservationists' fault. In fact, the louse's decline had probably been occurring in slow motion for the entire history of its host's decline. That's because feather lice, like the California condor louse, succeed or fail alongside their bird hosts. Nearly all bird species carry some feather lice, just like humans carry head lice. These tiny hitchhikers start their lives as **eggs** cemented to their host's feathers. After hatching, they spend their time

The California condor louse,
Colpocephalum californici

When they went extinct, dodos, moas, great
auks, Carolina parakeets, and passenger
pigeons brought many of their parasites
with them into oblivion.

munching feathers and hanging on for dear life, because if they lose hold of their host and fall off, death comes in a matter of minutes. In fact, these lice are so dependent on their hosts that each feather mite species can usually infect only one bird species. When your bird host's numbers are plunging from tens of thousands to thousands to twenty-two, that means fewer feathers to chew, and that means fewer feather mites. Secretly, without anyone noticing, the California condor louse was riding a bullet train to extinction, right alongside its host.

But thanks to the last-ditch rescue efforts of the conservationists, the California condor did not go extinct; in fact, the population has been steadily increasing, with nearly three hundred condors now living in the wild. And despite long odds against it, today's wild condors carry the same thing their parents and grandparents used to carry with them everywhere they went: their feather-mite friend. Phew, close call!

Sadly, many other lice have not been so lucky. That's because, if there is one thing that we humans are great at, it's driving species extinct. We especially excel at exterminating bird species. Ever petted a passenger pigeon? No, of course you haven't, because that species went extinct a hundred years before you were born. Ever doted on a dodo? Nope, that bird was gone a hundred years before your great-great-great-great-great-great-grandparents were born. How about Carolina parakeets, great auks, or giant moas? Nope, no, and nah.

The loss of these birds is a tragedy, but there's another, secret tragedy nested inside of each bird extinction: Every single one of these birds had feather mites (and other parasites) that could survive on no other host and that followed their bird host to oblivion—no delousing required. Because most parasites are unknown to science, these parasite species went extinct before they even got a name. At least we took the time to call a dodo a dodo before we wiped it off the face of the planet; no such respect was paid to the dodo's parasites.

Even today, we humans pay very little attention to the parasite species that we are condemning to extinction. One of the only parasites that is officially listed as "critically endangered" by the International Union for Conservation of Nature (IUCN, the folks who have the final word on what is endangered and what is not) is the hilariously named pygmy hog–sucking louse (the less-fun, scientific name is *Haematopinus oliveri*, pronounced heem-AT-oh-pine-us oh-live-AIR-i). As you might guess from the name, this louse sucks the blood of pygmy hogs, which are critically endangered themselves. But just because it has the lonely honor of being the only parasite on the official list of endangered

The critically endangered pygmy hog and its
critically endangered parasite, the
pygmy hog–sucking louse

species doesn't mean that it is the only parasite that is endangered. There are close to 130,000 species on the IUCN's list, with more than 35,000 getting pretty close to extinction. Every single one of those hosts has at least one parasite species that will follow it to its grave—and for the parasite, it will probably pass without even the dignity of getting a name.

This might sound like great news, right? Parasites do awful things to their hosts! They bore through brains, melt bones, gnaw feathers, suck blood! They're jerks! Shouldn't we celebrate the fact that we are wiping them off the face of the planet? Well, yes and no. Some parasites infect humans, causing awful **diseases** that can disable or kill us. You know by now that I love parasites, but even I can't condone that kind of behavior.

In contrast, the vast majority of parasite species want nothing to do with people. These parasites of wildlife might offend our sensibilities with their terrible manners (it's not polite to suck the blood of pygmy hogs at the dinner table, after all), but they are doing important work for ecosystems—keeping their host populations in check (as we'll see in chapters 7, 8, and 16) and sometimes even feeding the apex predators that we all adore (as we'll see in chapter 10). Without parasites, ecosystems would fall apart. The California condor louse narrowly avoided extinction, but many other parasites have not been so lucky—and that should worry us all.

~ 7 ~

ALIENS AMONG US

Speaking of **parasites** that want nothing at all to do with humans—let's talk about wasps. When I say "wasp," you probably think of the angry, black-and-yellow-striped stinging insects that swarm your soda can at picnics. But the family to which the wasps belong includes tens of thousands of species that make their living in a variety of ways—not just as picnic crashers. In fact, many wasps hate picnics, preferring instead to feast on the innards of other insects. We call these wasps **parasitoids**—a special name for animals with a special approach to being parasitic.

The parasitoid wasps have some nasty habits. Like every mom of every species, a parasitoid wasp mother wants only the best for her kids. Your mom might want you to live in a comfortable house or apartment, eat healthy food, and get along well with your siblings. A parasitoid wasp mom instead wants her wasp baby to live in a nice juicy caterpillar, eat nutritious caterpillar guts, and kill as many of its own brothers and sisters as possible. To each her own, I guess?

In order to achieve this happy life for her babies, a parasitoid wasp mom comes fully equipped. Instead of a stinger (like your picnic wasps might have), a parasitoid wasp female is outfitted with an organ called an ovipositor, which is like a long injection needle mounted on her butt. When she's ready to give birth, the parasitoid wasp mom flies out in search of a comfy home for her babies. Different kinds of parasitoid wasps select different homes for their kids: Some wasps love caterpillars (the larval stage of butterflies and moths); other wasps prefer to place their babies inside of aphids (tiny insects that you might find crawling over a cabbage plant in your backyard); yet other wasps find the greatest enjoyment inside of wriggly maggots (the larval stages of flies). But whatever insect **host** they choose, once the parasitoid wasp mom finds a suitable home for her babies, she uses her ovipositor to pierce the host's body and inject her **eggs** inside. The most gruesome part: The host doesn't die, at least not yet. Once she has finished laying her eggs, the female wasp flies off, leaving her brood behind.

"Phew!" the host exclaims, relieved that it has escaped with its life. Little does this poor insect know that its days are numbered, because even as it breathes a sigh of relief, the wasp babies are eating it from the inside out. The host might live for weeks afterward, doing all the things that it would normally do, including eating its normal foods and visiting its normal hangouts. But beneath the surface, things are anything but normal. Eventually, the wasp babies get big enough and hungry enough that they munch on one of the host's

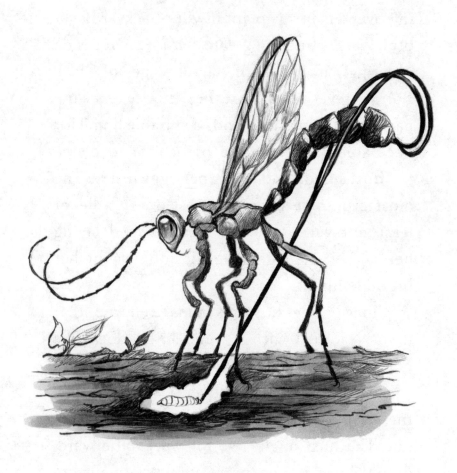

Female giant ichneumon wasp
using her ovipositor to drill through a tree's bark
and deposit eggs in a host hiding beneath

vital organs. Then the host dies and the babies emerge from the carcass to become adults themselves, finding hosts for their own babies to live within.

Let's consider the giant ichneumon (pronounced ICK-noo-mon) wasp, *Megarhyssa macrurus* (pronounced mega-RISS-uh mack-RUR-us). I choose this species because the giant ichneumon is, in my opinion, the most evil-looking of the parasitoid wasps. The female's ovipositor can be three times the length of her body. Although giant ichneumons look completely terrifying, they are harmless to people—fearsome only if you are a horntail. Horntails are a different kind of wasp, one that lays its own eggs under the bark of dead or dying trees. These eggs develop into larval **grubs**, which are the giant ichneumon's target. Giant ichneumon moms can sense horntail **larvae** under tree bark by using their antennae to detect the smell of horntails. Once a mom finds a horntail she likes, she uses the cutting tip on her ovipositor to drill through the tree bark all the way to the horntail larva, laying her egg within. These habits have earned the giant ichneumon the nickname of "stump stabber."

Although parasitoid wasps might seem like something out of a nightmare, farmers consider them to be trusted allies. That's because parasitoids are insect-killing machines, finely honed by evolution to search out and destroy their hosts. And those hosts are often farm pests, munching away on plants that farmers would otherwise harvest and sell. For example, aphids are a constant source of stress for farmers; these tiny insects don't look scary, but they suck plant juices, and their populations can grow rapidly, which spells disaster for crops—unless parasitoid wasps come to the rescue. There are many species of tiny parasitoid wasps adapted to exploit aphids. In fact, after these wasp babies infect their aphid host, they add insult to injury by turning the carcass of the host into a mummy. The aphid body swells up and develops a papery appearance— like the paper wrappings on human mummies found in Egypt. The wasp babies continue to develop safe and sound inside their aphid mummy, until they are ready to become adults. They then chew a hole in the mummy through which they can escape. In this morbid process, the wasps often kill enough aphids to prevent them from destroying a farmer's crop. As the old saying goes, "The enemy of my enemy is my friend."

Farmers aren't the only humans to find a good use for parasitoid wasps; Hollywood screenwriters have also found the parasitoids to be extremely useful. When you're all

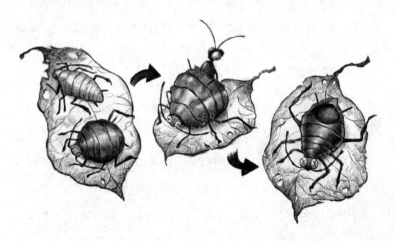

After "mummifying" their aphid
hosts, parasitoids emerge to
begin their adult lives.

grown up, I recommend that you watch the R-rated 1979 science-fiction film *Alien*. In that movie, humans exploring a crashed spaceship encounter an alien life-form that attacks one man, attaching itself to his face. I don't want to spoil the movie for future, grown-up you, but by now you're familiar with the parasitoids, so you'll probably be able to guess what happens next. More recently, the Netflix series *Stranger Things* featured another parasitoid—this one a creature from an alternate dimension that snakes its ovipositor down the throat of its host to insert its larvae. Clearly some Hollywood folks were paying close attention during biology class.

Of course the human-infecting parasitoids in *Alien* and *Stranger Things* are make-believe. There are no real-life parasitoids that can infect people. You could even argue that parasitoids are allies of people because, without the parasitoids, our food crops would be destroyed by pests. One of the coolest things about the parasitoids is their ability to control insect populations—to prevent the world from being overrun by caterpillars, aphids, or other insects that cause problems for people. But they are not the only parasites that can do this; other parasites can even control the abundance of much bigger hosts.

~ 8 ~

QUIT YOUR GROUSING

The Scottish Highlands are pretty spooky. In this lonely, cold, windswept, and mountainous place, the people are full of tall tales about murder, crime, and even ghosts. But the Scottish Highlands mystery that interests me most is 100 percent true: It's the mystery of the disappearing (and reappearing) grouse.

The red grouse is an iconic species. It is found only in the British Isles, and Scots slap its likeness on everything. It resembles a chicken with reddish brown feathers and a bright red comb right over its eye, which looks like a big fluffy eyebrow. Unlike barnyard chickens, grouse live out in the wild, and they are prized as a game bird, meaning that many people love nothing more than to spend their afternoons stalking these birds across the moors and then shooting them. Apparently, they're pretty tasty.

Because of the bird's value for hunting, every Scot wants grouse on their property, because more grouse means more afternoons of shooting with their buddies. In fact, folks who own large properties will often hire a full-time gamekeeper, whose responsibility is to make the annual hunts a success by increasing the number of grouse. That means making sure that the grouse have plenty of food and that poachers are kept out. It also means keeping very careful track of how many grouse are shot in each hunting season—also called keeping a "bag record," for the number of grouse that are "bagged." Generations of gamekeepers have kept bag records and, as a result, we have a very clear picture of what the red grouse has been up to over the past century. This is how we know that the grouse are doing something very strange indeed.

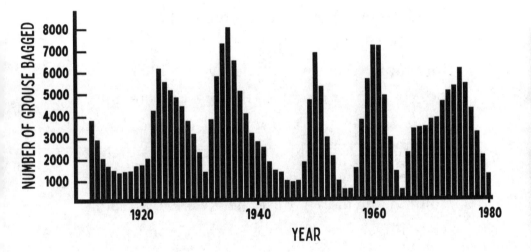

The number of grouse bagged on one moor
between 1911 and 1980

If you look at the bag record on the previous page, you'll see what I mean. Now comes the part of the book where I get to order you around! Ready? I want you to take your finger and put it in the lower left corner of the graph. Now trail your finger along the bottom of the graph from left to right. As you do that, you are moving from the deep past (starting in 1911) into more recent years (ending in 1980). Now put your finger on top of the first column, then move to the next column and onward down the graph. Each column represents the number of grouse bagged in one year—the taller the column, the more grouse there were. By tracing your finger over the tops of the columns, you will see how much change there was from one year to the next. The grouse seem to have very good years followed by very bad years, over and over again. How peculiar!

This boom-and-bust cycle frustrated gamekeepers. Sure, they got lots of credit for the great hunts in boom years. But when bust years came along, they couldn't explain to their bosses what had happened to the grouse. Just put yourself in the poor gamekeeper's shoes. You scrape most of the mud off your boots at the servant's entrance of a grand Scottish manor house and plod in, dreading what comes next. Wearily, you knock on the door to your boss's study. You explain to the great lord that grouse are sparse this year and that His Lordship's upcoming hunt might need to be canceled. You accept the tongue-lashing that comes. But no matter how red in the face m'lord becomes, it doesn't create more grouse—it'll still be a bad year to go shooting.

Gamekeepers tried to solve this puzzle for years. Low grouse numbers didn't seem to be related to food; the tender plant shoots that the grouse snack on were just as abundant in bust years as they were in boom years. And it also didn't seem to be related to hunting, because the same number of birds were shot in the few years before a boom as in the few years before a bust. The gamekeepers were desperate: Why did the grouse disappear every few years, only to mysteriously reappear? If the situation didn't improve quickly, a gamekeeper could be fired.

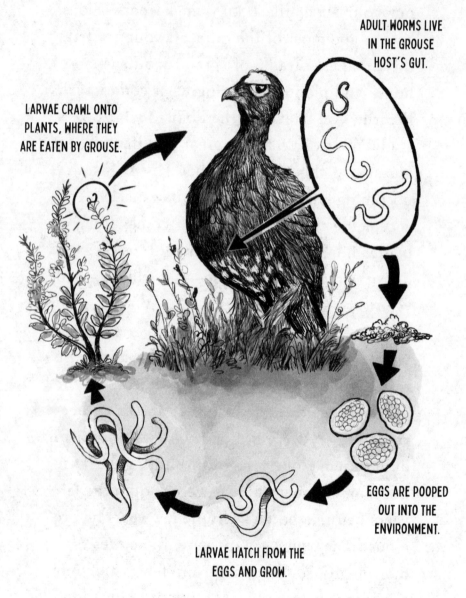

ADULT WORMS LIVE
IN THE GROUSE
HOST'S GUT.

LARVAE CRAWL ONTO
PLANTS, WHERE THEY
ARE EATEN BY GROUSE.

EGGS ARE POOPED
OUT INTO THE
ENVIRONMENT.

LARVAE HATCH FROM THE
EGGS AND GROW.

Life cycle of Trichostrongylus tenuis

Or worse: What if the lord thought the game-keeper had stolen all the birds for himself?

Well, as you might have guessed, the key to this mystery lies in **parasitology**. What the game-keepers didn't know during all those generations of booming and busting grouse was that a puppet master was pulling the strings behind the scenes. That puppet master was a worm—the grouse worm, *Trichostrongylus tenuis* (pronounced trick-oh-STRON-jill-uss TEN-you-iss), to be exact. These **parasites** live in the guts of red grouse, where they have the irritating habit of burrowing into the walls of the intestine. Once comfortably tucked in, the worms pair up to raise their families. Worm couples produce **eggs** in the gut tract, and those eggs are pooped out into the environment, where they hatch to produce tiny grouse worm **larvae**. Even though they are mere babies, grouse worm larvae are smart and resourceful; they crawl up to the top of the tender plant shoots that the birds love to munch, where they are eaten by an unsuspecting grouse. Once in the intestine of their new **host**, they can mate and begin the life cycle all over again.

The worms don't want to kill their hosts—after all, if the grouse dies, the worm dies, too. But despite the worms' best efforts, they can't help but make the infected grouse hungrier, chillier, and stinkier than healthy birds, which can get them killed even before hunters have a chance to shoot them. Infected grouse are less hardy against the harsh winter weather and tend to drop dead from the cold. They need more food to feed themselves plus the worm families growing inside them. The infection also intensifies the grousy smell of grouse, making it easier for predators like foxes to find and eat infected grouse. (I have never sniffed either an infected or an uninfected grouse, but grouse body odor has been measured by science, and science tells us that infected grouse are indeed stinkier. Yes, some poor soul spent years sniffing grouse armpits—and one day that could be you!)

Here's where it gets good. Remember that boom-and-bust cycle that ticked off Lord McWhatsHisFace and bummed out the gamekeeper? Well, there is a perfectly logical explanation for why it occurs. During boom years, as grouse increase in numbers, they are quietly transmitting more and more parasites to one another. That's because the more birds there are, the more resources there are for the parasites to use, and the more reproduction the parasites can accomplish. Eventually, there are too many parasites, and they begin to accidentally kill the birds. As more birds die, we end up with a bust year—and our poor gamekeeper gets in trouble. Because so many grouse are dying parasite-related deaths, there are now fewer grouse, and it is harder for the parasites to transmit among grouse. As a result, infection goes down. Released from the crushing burden of parasitic infection, the grouse can now increase. And so on, forever!

Sure, witches and ghosts and haunted Scottish manor houses are spooky. But all these things come from the imaginations of people. Real life is way spookier. What's more sinister than finding out that secretive parasites hiding in the intestines of grouse were pulling the strings all along?

9

GHOSTS
OF HOSTS PAST

Do you ever wonder what it would be like to time travel? I sometimes imagine myself strolling through Victorian London in the mid-1800s, or voyaging with Polynesian navigators in the year 1000, or hiding from saber-toothed cats in my prehistoric cave. The funny thing is this: Even if I were able to transport myself through time, I would not be able to escape from **parasites**. Parasitism is not a modern phenomenon. Parasites have been with us for millions of years. And through all the radical changes that Earth has experienced in that time, the parasites have managed to devise clever tricks for surviving.

Consider the extinction of the dinosaurs. We tend to have a pretty rosy view of this event—after all, the age of the dinosaurs had to pass before mammals (like us!) could inherit the Earth. But the event that brought on the downfall of dinos was an absolute catastrophe for anyone who happened to be living on the planet at the time. About sixty-six million years ago, a massive asteroid collided with Earth, smashing into present-day Mexico. The asteroid itself was between six and nine miles wide, and it hit the planet with such force that it left behind a crater more than one hundred miles wide. Chemicals from the impact caused rain, rivers, streams, and oceans to turn to acid. Much of Earth's surface was engulfed in flames. Soot from these fires and dust from the impact blocked out the sun for almost a year. With no sun, plants could not survive and, with no plants, animals could not survive. In darkness, Earth's entire surface plunged below freezing. Those **organisms** not pummeled by debris, cooked by radiation, melted by acid, or frozen to death had starvation to look forward to. Unsurprisingly, three out of every four species on the planet went extinct. I'm glad that humans don't have to share Earth with *Tyrannosaurus rex*, but my heart goes out to any creature whose happy home suddenly turns into an acid fireball of death.

The asteroid that collided with Earth at the end of the Cretaceous period doomed the dinosaurs and marine reptiles, along with some of their parasites.

Among the many creatures that did not make it were the mosasaurs. Marine reptiles related to the modern-day lizards and snakes, mosasaurs ran the oceans during the late Cretaceous period. These terrifying marine predators could clock in at up to fifty feet in length. Fifty feet—that's about the size of a humpback whale! But where the humpback peacefully sieves **krill** out of ocean waters, the mosasaur voraciously hunted **ammonites**, fish, birds—and sometimes other mosasaurs. If they lived today, no one would dare to dip a toe in the ocean.

Although these top predators seemed to be kings and queens of Cretaceous oceans, there was one group of organisms that held sway over the mosasaurs: their parasites. It's tricky to learn about the parasites of extinct **hosts**, because parasites are soft-bodied and so they tend not to be preserved as **fossils**. The things that fossilize well are bone, cartilage, sometimes scales—but not mushy, gooey, slimy parasites. That said, some creative **parasitologists** have used modern-day parasites to learn about what might have been eating the mosasaurs while the mosasaurs were busy eating everything else.

And with that, we come to my very favorite parasite: *Amphilina foliacea* (pronounced am-fuh-LINE-uh foal-ee-A-see-uh). This parasite has no common name, so instead of repeating that Latin mouthful over and over, I'm just going to use my personal pet name for it from here on: "amphie." By now you've figured out that I like weird stuff. I find it boring when things, people, species are all the same, so I'm always drawn toward whatever is different, unusual, unique. And amphie is weird even among all the weirdo parasites you've read about so far.

Here are the things that make amphie unique:

1. Amphie is a tapeworm, but it doesn't look anything like a normal tapeworm. Typical adult tapeworms look like a long strand of unspooled tape. But amphie just looks like a simple oval.

2. Amphie's life cycle is missing a bunch of steps that we would expect to see in a normal tapeworm life cycle.

3. Amphie's larval stages are capable of sexual reproduction—which is the equivalent of a five-year-old human having a baby.

Yikes, that's a lot of weirdness for one little worm!

So what on God's green Earth happened to make amphie so unusual? We'll never know for sure, because humans weren't around to observe amphie as it evolved over the past several million years. But we have a pretty good guess, and it has to do with that mega asteroid that wiped out the dinosaurs.

To explain, I first need to describe how a normal tapeworm life cycle works. It all starts with a large **vertebrate** animal, often a shark, sometimes a mammal, bird, or reptile, that carries **adult** tapeworms in its gut. Those adult tapeworms mate and produce **eggs**. The eggs are pooped out, perhaps into the ocean, where they hatch. The hatched **larvae** go on to infect a very different host species, usually a tiny **crustacean** floating in the **plankton** or

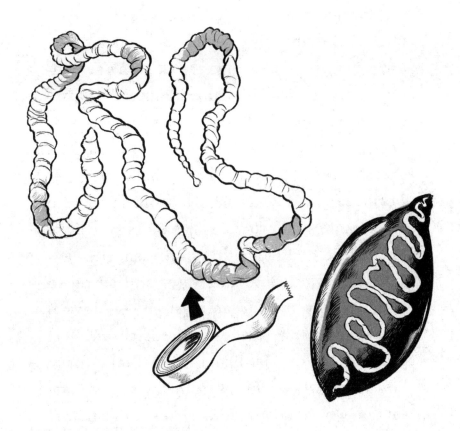

Typical adult tapeworm (left) and Amphilina
foliacea, *or amphie (right). As the name suggests,
tapeworms usually look like a long strand of
unspooled tape. But* amphie *just looks
like a simple oval. What gives?*

skittering along the ocean bottom. That tiny crustacean then gets eaten by a fish. You might think that this would spell curtains for the tapeworm, but things are all going according to the parasite's plan, because the larval tapeworm doesn't die. It instead infects that unsuspecting fish. When the fish is eaten by a shark or other large vertebrate host, the tapeworm can finally transform from larva into adult, mate, and produce eggs of its very own.

Amphie does something different. Its eggs are pooped out into the water and go on to infect a tiny crustacean, just like a normal tapeworm. And that tiny crustacean gets eaten by a fish, just like a normal tapeworm. But here's where things go haywire. The larval tapeworm hanging out inside the fish host mates and starts producing eggs of its own, and it's the fish host that releases the eggs into the ocean. Where did that big vertebrate host go? How did amphie manage to short-circuit the most important part of the tapeworm life cycle?

Scientists think that amphie might have

originally been a normal, boring tapeworm parasite of . . . you guessed it, mosasaurs. It would
have had a normal, boring tapeworm life cycle;
it would have looked like a normal, boring
adult tapeworm in the mosasaur gut; and it

*Normal tapeworm life cycle (left), amphie's life
cycle today (center), amphie's life cycle in the
Cretaceous period (right)*

would never have done any of the precocious
reproductive behaviors that we observe today.
But then the asteroid hit and *POW!* Mosasaurs
were gone. What could amphie do? It might
have followed its host into extinction—there
were probably many other parasite species
that went down that path. But amphie did

something different. It evolved the ability to sexually reproduce in its larval stage, eliminating any need for the mosasaur host, and leaving us with the oddball parasite that we know and love today. Amphie's uniqueness is a scar—a mark left on it forever by a catastrophic event. But amphie's uniqueness is also a symbol of its resilience; without these bizarre adaptations, amphie would have followed its fellow Cretaceous parasites into extinction.

Everyone knows that the extinction of the dinosaurs and marine reptiles was a big deal. But amphie highlights the fact that it wasn't just hulking reptiles that went extinct when that asteroid crashed into Earth. Many of the parasites that infected those reptiles probably went extinct alongside their hosts. Amphie is a survivor of that mega-extinction event, a relic of a time when dinosaurs—not humans—ruled Earth. And it is a reminder that, no matter how far back in time you travel, there will always be parasites lurking in the background, waiting for their opportunity to strike.

10

BODY SNATCHERS

Science fiction is full of stories of people who lose their free will to some evil force. Zombies used to be people, but after zombification they think about nothing but eating brains. Vampires used to be people, but after that fateful bite, they think of nothing but drinking blood. Werewolves can't control their transformation; whether they like it or not, the full moon makes a violent beast out of an otherwise gentle person. While zombies, vampires, and werewolves are not real (to my knowledge, anyway), there are real-life **parasites** that can cause disturbing transformations in their **hosts**.

Consider the nematomorph (pronounced

nem-A-toh-morf). This worm is capable of doing something so nefarious, so tricky, so downright evil, that if it were a human it would be jailed forever. Luckily, it's a nematomorph and its hosts are insects, so it has escaped prosecution.

Nematomorphs are only parasitic in their larval stages; the **adult** nematomorph lives out in the environment on its own. Adult nematomorphs can be found in freshwater streams on every continent except Antarctica, so it is possible that nematomorphs are wriggling around in a stream near you (unless you're living at an Antarctic research station—and, in that case, can I come visit you?). The adults mate in shallow streams and deposit **eggs**, which hatch and are ingested by insects like crickets when they drink water from that stream. Once inside the insect host, the larval parasite grows and matures, eventually becoming so big that it can get quite crowded against the insect's organs (just like the **parasitoid** wasp babies in chapter 7).

Now is the moment when the nematomorph

AFTER BEING CONSUMED BY THE
CRICKET, THE LARVAE MATURE INTO
ADULTS INSIDE THEIR CRICKET HOST.

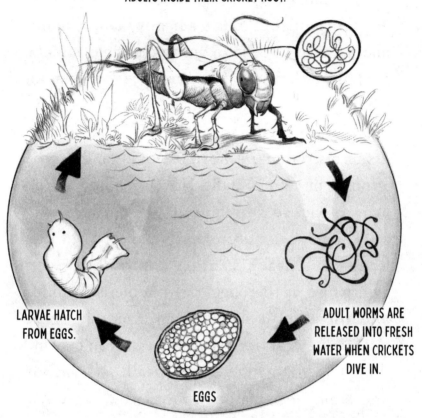

LARVAE HATCH
FROM EGGS.

EGGS

ADULT WORMS ARE
RELEASED INTO FRESH
WATER WHEN CRICKETS
DIVE IN.

An insect host can become infected by drinking
nematomorph larvae in water, and after the
larva has grown inside it, the host will return the
parasite to water by jumping in.

goes from just plain bad guy to evil genius. The nematomorph larva is inside an insect, which lives on land. But to live a happy adult nematomorph life, it needs to get to a puddle, stream, or pond, where it can swim, meet other adult nematomorphs, pick a mate, and start a family. If the nematomorph merely broke out of its terrestrial insect host, it would land on the ground, dry out, and die. How is it going to find its way back to a stream?

The nematomorphs have come up with an extremely sneaky solution. Normally, insects will pause at the edge of a puddle, stream, or pond to drink water but will avoid falling in. After all, most terrestrial insects can't swim, so going for a dip equals death. But inside the mind of nematomorph-infected insects, a strange idea takes hold. These infected hosts find themselves drawn to water, wandering toward it, pondering it, and eventually jumping right in. This is suicide for the insect, because the host's compulsion to jump into water often means death by drowning. But it's great for the nematomorph, who has just convinced the insect host to serve as a limousine service, ferrying the parasite to its desired habitat in style. After the host's last swan dive, the nemato-morph larva senses water and breaks out of the host's exoskeleton, emerging into the aquatic environment to begin its adult life.

Using mind control to force your host to take its own life is pretty evil but not uncom-mon among the parasites. Another worm can do something similar. *Dicrocoelium dendriti-cum* (pronounced die-crow-SEEL-ee-um den-DRIT-ick-um), or the lancet liver fluke, has a **complex life cycle**. Its adult stage is found in animals that eat grass, especially sheep and cows. Sheep and cow hosts poop out the par-asite's eggs onto the grass, where they are ingested by land snails. Infected snails cough up slime balls full of parasite **larvae**, which ants find delectable. It is only after the ants chow down on snail slime balls and become infected that the real magic begins.

Normally, ants spend their days gathering food and their nights snuggled in their nests with all of their ant siblings. But ants infected

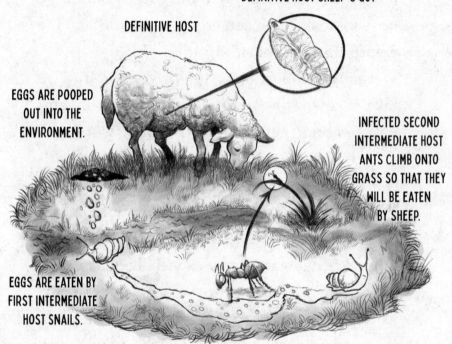

ADULT PARASITE LIVING IN THE
DEFINITIVE HOST SHEEP'S GUT

DEFINITIVE HOST

EGGS ARE POOPED
OUT INTO THE
ENVIRONMENT.

INFECTED SECOND
INTERMEDIATE HOST
ANTS CLIMB ONTO
GRASS SO THAT THEY
WILL BE EATEN
BY SHEEP.

EGGS ARE EATEN BY
FIRST INTERMEDIATE
HOST SNAILS.

LARVAE ARE DEPOSITED IN THE SNAIL'S
SLIME TRAIL, WHICH IS EATEN BY SECOND
INTERMEDIATE HOST ANTS.

Dicrocoelium dendriticum *life cycle*

with the lancet liver fluke pull a night shift. They behave like normal ants during the day but, as night falls, they peel away from the crowd of ants streaming back to the nest. They wander off alone, climb up a blade of grass, bite onto the tip of that blade of grass, and hang there all night long. As the sun comes up, they snap out of their trance, wander back down the blade of grass, and rejoin their comrades for the day's ant activities.

Why does the lancet liver fluke force its ant host to do this freaky nighttime ritual? For the same reason that the nematomorph makes its insect host jump into water: It wants to get to the right habitat. By hanging on a blade of grass, the ant is making it possible for a sheep to accidentally ingest it as it grazes, and that is exactly what the lancet liver fluke wants. This activity has to happen at night, because if the ant and its parasite were to hang out on grass blades during the day, they would get too hot and both the ant and its parasite would die. But by hanging out on the grass blades in the cool of the evening, the parasite can ensure that one day, eventually, the ant will get eaten by a sheep with the midnight munchies. Once the lancet liver fluke gets into its sheep host, it can become an adult and continue its life cycle. The parasite forces its ant host to get itself eaten. This is a behavior that is very much not in the ant's best interest, but the parasite can somehow force it to do the behavior anyway—almost like the parasite has turned the ant into a zombie!

I have one more example. Nematomorphs and lancet liver flukes manipulate their hosts' behavior to get what they want, but other parasites can actually change their hosts' appearance. *Leucochloridium paradoxum* (pronounced loo-ko-klor-ID-ee-um par-uh-DOX-um), also called the green-banded broodsac, is closely related to the lancet liver fluke but has a very different effect on its host. Its larval stages live in a land snail, and it reaches its adult stage in birds. To maximize the success of its larval parasites in their quest to get into the gut of birds, the parasite takes matters into its own hands (or suckers, as the case may be). The

ADULT WORM IN THE
GUT OF THE DEFINITIVE
HOST BIRD

EGGS ARE POOPED
OUT INTO THE
ENVIRONMENT.

EGGS ARE EATEN
BY INTERMEDIATE
HOST SNAILS.

DEFINITIVE HOST BIRDS
EAT THE INFECTED
SNAILS AND BECOME
INFECTED THEMSELVES.

PARASITE LARVAE CHANGE THE APPEARANCE
OF THE SNAIL HOST'S TENTACLE.

Leucochloridium paradoxum *life cycle*

larval parasites crawl into the tentacles of the snail, making them swell and pulsate. These tentacles become brilliantly colored, and the overall appearance of the infected tentacle mimics that of a caterpillar—a favorite food of birds. By making its host's tentacles extremely visible, the parasite increases the likelihood that it will wind up in a bird's gut—exactly where it needs to be.

I'm convinced that science fiction writers aren't writing fiction at all. The stories they tell about zombies, vampires, and werewolves are not far-fetched. In nature, horror movie plots play out in real life: suicidal crickets, zombified ants, grotesque and deadly ornaments on a snail's head. But can this stuff happen to humans? In the next section, we'll discuss some parasites that are closer to home and find out whether the same nefarious parasites we've met in wild hosts can be found in your home, your food, your pets, or you.

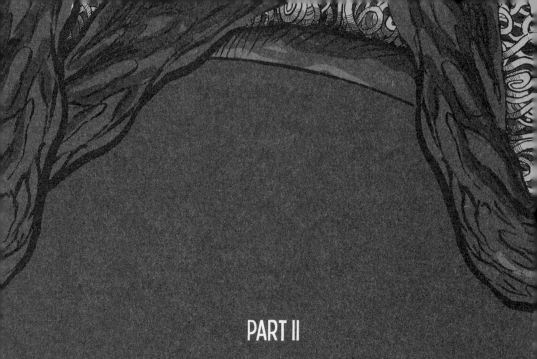

PART II

PARASITES IN YOUR HOME, YOUR FOOD, YOUR PETS, AND YOU

~ 11 ~

A PLAGUE ON BOTH YOUR HOUSES

Perhaps you remember the COVID-19 pandemic and, if you do, you know something that humans throughout history have known: how awful it is to live through a **plague**. COVID-19 is not the first **disease** to sweep across the world, leaving millions dead. In fact, plagues have been so common and devastating throughout human history that they are memorialized in an uncountable number of books, poems, songs, and plays. In Shakespeare's *Romeo and Juliet*,

Mercutio gets super angry after being stabbed with a sword (I'd be ticked off, too!), and the most hateful curse he can summon against the people responsible is "A plague o' both your houses!" The houses he's talking about are those of the Montagues and the Capulets, the families whose nonstop feuding leads to the street fight in which Mercutio is fatally wounded. As he lies bleeding to death, Mercutio wishes on these people the worst thing he can imagine: disease.

There is one particular disease that Mercutio probably had in mind. At the time Shakespeare wrote his plays, the world had just lived through the worst of the black death, which kicked off in the mid-1300s. Creepy name, right? Well, it should sound creepy, because by some estimates, this massive pandemic killed one out of every three people living in Europe at the time.

Imagine for a moment that I have magically teleported you back to medieval Europe. The year is 1348. As dawn breaks, you rise from a bed of straw, which you share with your three siblings, and head out the front door. It's a warm, early-summer morning, and as you dawdle down the cobbled street enjoying the sunshine, you pass chickens, goats, sheep, cows, dogs, and cats doing the same. An open gutter alongside the road carries raw sewage down to the harbor, but you're in luck: You've risen early enough that you will miss the sight of your neighbor squatting over the gutter's edge to make his daily contribution to this stream of filth. Finally, you arrive at the marketplace across from the waterfront, where huge ships from distant places unload their cargo. You hand over a coin to the baker, select a loaf of bread for your family's breakfast, and turn back toward home.

This routine is a familiar one, but today, you can tell that something new is happening. As you walk home, you see a neighbor family hauling a dead body out of their house and dropping it with a thud into an open cart waiting in the street. Curious, you approach the cart, only to find that the corpse has several egg-sized lumps on his neck, each of which oozes a mixture of pus and blood, and his fingers and toes are blackened as if they've been burned.

"That's unusual," you think to yourself, and walk on. Closer to home, you find your aunt staggering toward her own house. She's having so much trouble walking, you take her hand to escort her and immediately notice that her skin is burning hot. As you drag her along, she doubles over, spewing bloody vomit on the cobblestones. Within a week, you discover a lump on your own neck—and having seen this before, you know what is coming for you.

As your present-day self might have guessed, all of this misery was caused by a teeny tiny **parasite**: a bacterium whose scientific name is *Yersinia pestis* (pronounced yer-SIN-ee-uh PESS-tiss). People can be infected by this bacterium in several ways, including by breathing in airborne droplets (like those produced by the cough or sneeze of an infected person) and through the bite of an infected flea. In medieval Europe, fleas were a fact of life; if you had lived at that time, instead of teaching you to say "please" and "thank you," your parents would have taught you that it isn't polite to pick fleas off yourself at the dinner table. Sure, you could squash a flea to death between your fingers any other time, but certainly not during a family supper. Perhaps parents should have relaxed their etiquette rules, because the bite of a flea could mean death—but no one knew that until long after the black death had passed.

So what in the world was going wrong in that medieval city I sent you to a few paragraphs ago? Well, remember the ships moored across from the baker's shop at the waterfront marketplace? During its travels, one of those ships had acquired some stowaways. Rats can climb the ropes used to tether boats to a dock, and, in the last port of call, some of those wily rodents had manage to sneak aboard; once they reached your city, they decided that it was a good place to disembark. The rats carried the plague bacterium, and they also carried rat fleas. Fleas are tiny insects that live in the hair, fur, or feathers of their **hosts**, feeding on the host's blood. When that blood contains the plague bacterium, fleas become infected.

But how does plague get from rats at the waterfront to humans in the city? Well, the rats abandoned ship, scurrying ashore by tightrope-walking the dock lines, and then they fanned out and took up residence in homes. Some of the rat fleas hopped off the rats and onto the people living alongside them. With all the animals, garbage, and human waste lying around, finding rats in the house would not have been unusual. But once an infected rat flea makes the jump to a human, things get very unusual very quickly. The plague bacterium does something pretty evil to infected rat fleas: It plugs up the gut tract of the flea, making it impossible for the flea to digest and poop out the blood that it consumes. With nowhere else to go, the partially digested blood in the flea's gut has to come out somewhere, so it gets barfed up by the flea—along with plenty of plague **bacteria**. When an infected rat flea bites a person, it then pukes out a bunch of plague bacteria into the wound, ensuring that that person will become infected by plague. An infected person can therefore infect others in two ways: (1) by coughing, or (2) by getting bitten by fleas, which then hop off the infected human to bite new hosts. You might have gotten infected by a cough from your aunt or by a flea fleeing the corpse in the cart. Given the crowded and unsanitary conditions in medieval Europe, it would have been very difficult indeed for most people to avoid becoming infected.

Xenopsylla cheopis, *the rat flea responsible for transmission of the plague bacterium* Yersinia pestis *to people during the black death*

~ ✸ ~

That's how a healthy, thriving city became a plague-infested bedlam. Quarantines were placed on incoming ships, but this measure failed to stop the rapid spread of plague, which had already made landfall. Newcomers to a city were required to isolate themselves for more than a month after their arrival, but this measure was also too little, too late. So many people died that there were not enough undertakers to bury the bodies individually and many wound up in mass graves. Entire families were struck down simultaneously. People who had the resources to leave abandoned their city residences for the countryside, where there was less infection, but the fleeing urbanites brought plague with them wherever they went. Plague ravaged Asia, the Middle East, Northern Africa, and Europe for hundreds of years, and it still pops up sporadically today, even though we have insecticides to kill fleas, rodenticides to kill rodents, antibiotics to kill the plague bacterium in the human body, and even a vaccine against plague. As recently as 2017, over 200 people died in a plague outbreak in Madagascar. Plague still circulates between rodents and fleas (and occasionally humans) in the western United States.

The story of plague should sound familiar to those of us who know the COVID-19 pandemic: the sudden appearance and rapid spread of a strange new illness, orders from the government to stay indoors, fear and panic as people try to protect their friends, families, and themselves. Humans have been living with pandemic parasites for a long time. This long history suggests to me that COVID-19 is not the last pestilence that humanity will face.

~ 12 ~

WAITER, THERE'S A WORM IN MY SUSHI!

Does the idea of swallowing cold raw fish make your mouth water? Me too! But what if I told you that live worms might be hiding inside that delicious bite of salmon roll, hitching a ride straight to your intestine?

Meet the sushi worms! These worms include many species (the most common are *Anisakis simplex* [pronounced an-ih-SACK-us SIM-plex] and *Pseudoterranova decipiens* [pronounced soo-doh-terr-ih-NO-va duh-SIP-ee-ens]), which are found all over the world in many different kinds of ocean fish. And they are a problem for people who enjoy eating seafood dishes that are uncooked, pickled, or smoked. That includes pickled anchovies and herring, ceviche, sushi, and sashimi. All of these delicacies can conceal living sushi worms, which wreak havoc in the human intestine. They are small enough that they can pass through the mouth undamaged by chomping teeth. They then pass through the stomach and into the intestine, where they set up shop. If you're really unlucky, the worms might burrow through your intestinal lining, puncturing the intestine and allowing small amounts of poop to leak onto your other organs. I probably don't need to tell you that this is bad.

But even if the worms behave and don't puncture the intestine, they can still cause a lot of trouble. That's because the presence of the worms causes a person's **immune system** to kick into high gear. The immune system recognizes the worm as a threat and wants to destroy it. It sends immune **cells** to attack the worm.

Sushi worms

Most of the time, it is the fury of the immune system—not the worm itself—that causes the symptoms of vomiting, diarrhea, and tummy ache. The worm can't reproduce in a human intestine, so eventually it dies and its limp wormy carcass gets passed out of the body in poop.

This is a sad story for the human **host**, but it's also a sad story for the **parasite**. Why? Because the sushi worm didn't get to fulfill its mission of making baby sushi worms! It failed in its life's work because these worms are not meant to be in the human intestine. People are just an "accidental" host—collateral damage in the worm's quest to reproduce. Sushi worms are meant to live in the intestines of whales, dolphins, seals, and sea lions. They have a ridiculously **complex life cycle** that takes them from the very bottom of the ocean food web to the very top, with occasional detours into people.

The life cycle of the sushi worm begins when it is pooped out of a marine mammal host. It hatches in the water and is consumed by a **crustacean**, like **krill**. The krill thinks it has just gotten a delicious meal, but what it doesn't know is that it has fallen right into the parasite's trap. The sushi worm busts through the krill's intestinal wall and swims around inside its body, happy as a clam. Now the worm is ready for the next stage of its life. When its krill host gets eaten by a fish, the sushi worm is delighted! It bursts through the intestine of the fish and settles down in the fish's muscles, again happy to have successfully made the leap into its next host. Now all the sushi worm has to do is wait for its fish host to be eaten by a dolphin, and it has hit the jackpot. It finds a mate in the dolphin's intestine, lays **eggs**, and the cycle can begin all over again. Mission accomplished! But there is one big, dangerous wrong turn in the life of the sushi worm that it wants to avoid at all costs: being accidentally eaten by a human. Humans get involved in this life cycle when they eat a fish that the worm was hoping might instead get gobbled up by a dolphin. Landing in the human intestine is game over for this parasite.

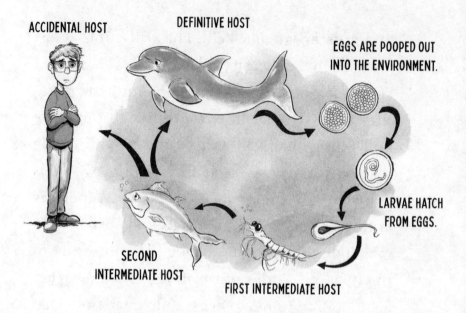

ACCIDENTAL HOST

DEFINITIVE HOST

EGGS ARE POOPED OUT
INTO THE ENVIRONMENT.

LARVAE HATCH
FROM EGGS.

SECOND
INTERMEDIATE HOST

FIRST INTERMEDIATE HOST

Life cycle of Anisakis simplex

How do you know if you are playing host to a sushi worm? Most people never find out. That's because the symptoms of infection closely mimic the symptoms of food poisoning. And usually when folks find themselves barfing, passing copious amounts of diarrhea, or doubled over with stomach pain after a dinner of raw fish, they blame it on "bad sushi." These episodes pass after a few days and people move on with their lives. And sometimes, the illness really is food poisoning—that is, bad bacteria that grew on the fish because it wasn't frozen or refrigerated at the proper temperatures. But sometimes, all that vomit is the result of just a single measly worm, trying in vain to make its home in your intestine.

The only way to know for sure that you are infected with a sushi worm is pretty unpleasant, so it is usually only done for patients whose symptoms linger for weeks. A doctor will give you medicine to put you to sleep and then pass a camera on a long cord down your throat, into your stomach, and through your intestine, in a procedure called endoscopy. (Translated from Latin, this word means "seeing inside.") The camera lights up your insides and records video of the action in your intestine. Like a deep-sea submersible, this camera comes equipped with grabbers (think: the claw hand used to retrieve stuffed animals in an arcade game) that the doctor can manipulate, so that when she finds your worm, she can nab it and pull it out of your body. Endoscopy is an expensive and unpleasant medical procedure that is usually avoided, particularly for people who just experience a few days of vomiting and then start feeling better—which is why so many people never find out that they played host to a sushi worm!

The most common question I am asked by students who are new to the study of parasites is, "Do you still eat seafood?" My answer? "Of course I do!" A few stray worms will never put me off raw fish. Besides, the risk of encountering a worm is low and, if you do encounter one, the risk of getting sick is low, too. I'll take the tiny risk of puking later on in the evening if it means that I can enjoy some delicious nigiri for dinner. In fact, I'm kind of delighted by the thought that eating these worms connects me to a grand cycle linking the very lowliest species in an ocean food web (like krill) to the most majestic (like whales).

For that same reason, I will even eat raw oysters, which can get infected with a worm several times the size of the puny sushi worm...

BLISSFUL BLISTERS

Eating raw oysters isn't everyone's cup of tea, but I love them. If you order oysters in a restaurant, the server will bring you a big tray filled with crushed ice. Nestled into that ice you'll find a dozen half shells, each cupping a gooey lump of oyster flesh. I like to pick up the shell, tilt it into my mouth, and slurp the oyster down as fresh and raw as possible, as if I just grabbed it from the ocean myself. Other folks will add a condiment like cocktail sauce before slurping. But whichever way you go about the slurp, eating a raw oyster is like getting hit in the face by a wave—there's no mistaking the wild, briny taste of the sea.

One of the other lovely things about eating oysters is that, even if you've requested a table for one, you're never truly dining alone. That's because oysters all over the world play **host** to shell-boring **parasites**, which will keep you company as long as the oysters last.

Rows of oyster bags on an oyster farm: Lines are strung up in the intertidal zone in rows; dangling on lines are "tumble bags" filled with oysters.

Like clams and mussels, oysters are members of a group of animals called the **bivalves**. Bivalves have hinged shells with two halves that fit together like a book's cover. Before an oyster is served up on a tray of crushed ice, the two shell halves (called valves) are pried apart and the animal inside is laid on one valve to be presented to a hungry customer. Any oyster on your plate will have grown up in one of two places: in the wild or on an oyster farm. The word "farm" might conjure up images of neat rows of crops, and oyster farms are much the same. One way to grow them is for oyster farmers to take baby oysters, put them into bags, and suspend them in ocean water so that they can grow up to be big, strong, and delicious. But this time spent in the ocean (whether in the wild or on a farm) is also a time when oysters can pick up unwanted hitchhikers.

Meet the shell-boring polychaetes, worms who drill tunnels into oyster shells to make safe, cozy homes for themselves. Like their oyster hosts, these worms are found all over the world; in fact, they have been found in every major oyster-growing region. Until recently, scientists thought that my home—the US Pacific Northwest—was free of these parasites. But when my lab group started looking, sure enough we found them here, too. Lucky for us (yay, more parasites to study!), but not so lucky for the oysters (boo, shells full of wormholes).

These polychaetes are particularly well-adapted to their unusual lifestyle. Baby shell-boring polychaetes are so tiny that they are not visible to the naked eye—you'll need a microscope to see them—and they usually live in the **plankton**, floating happily along with the ocean currents. When it's time to get serious and grow into an **adult** worm, they find an oyster shell to settle down on. That's when the worm gets to work, secreting chemicals to dissolve the oyster shell bit by bit so that it can excavate a tunnel from the outside in. This tunnel is typically U-shaped so that the worm can stick its head out of one hole to feed and its butt out of another hole to poop. Not the classiest move, but it gets the job done.

Here's where things get bad for the oyster host. As the worm grows, it needs to make a bigger and bigger tunnel to accommodate its growing body. The worm excavates more and more oyster shell, causing its tunnel to go from

*A shell-boring polychaete pokes its head out of
its tunnel to feed on detritus. These worms will
also steal food from their oyster hosts—usually
plankton that the oyster has filtered
out of the water.*

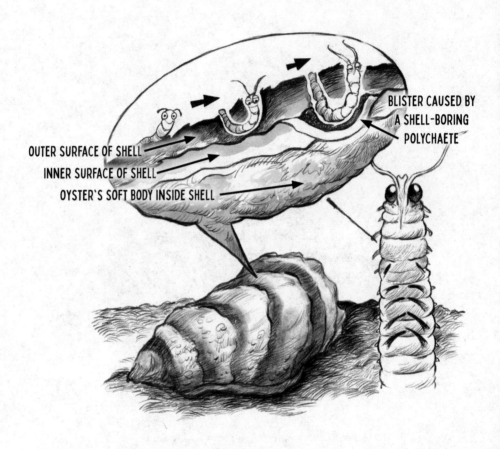

OUTER SURFACE OF SHELL

INNER SURFACE OF SHELL

OYSTER'S SOFT BODY INSIDE SHELL

BLISTER CAUSED BY A SHELL-BORING POLYCHAETE

A small U-shaped burrow can grow into a large U-shaped burrow that breaches the inner surface of the oyster valve, prompting the oyster to build a blister.

a tiny, lowercase "u" that is totally contained inside the hard part of the oyster's shell to a big, honking uppercase "U" that breaches the inner surface of the oyster's shell at the curve in the "U." Now the worm is in contact with the oyster's soft body, which the host finds super disturbing. To keep its gooey, delicate body safe from the worm, the oyster puts its shell-production gear into overdrive and builds a hard, pearly layer of shell between itself and the worm. (Incidentally, this shell-production response is the same process that makes pearls—except in the case of a pearl, the oyster is laying down the hard, pearly material on a stray bit of junk, like sand, that has gotten inside the oyster shell.) The result of all this panicky shell production is that the oyster creates a blister on the inner surface of its own shell, which keeps the worm away from the oyster's body. Worms don't talk, but if they could, they'd now say, "Killer, dude! Extra space to store my dirt and poop collection!" No sooner is this blister created than the worm sets to work filling it up with dirt and poop, creating a spacious home to mate and spew its babies into the plankton.

These tunnels and blisters are not great for oyster hosts for a few reasons. First, the more tunnels in a shell, the more brittle and breakable it is. The shell is a shield protecting the soft-bodied oyster from being eaten by a predator, so the oyster wants it to be as strong as possible; shell-boring worms undermine that goal. Second, the oyster has to spend a lot of its energy to protect itself against the worms; pearls and blisters are made of materials that cost the oyster a lot of energy to make, and if it didn't have to make those costly things, the oyster could put its energy toward growing bigger or making more oyster babies.

Neither is the worm very good for the oyster farmer. This is because—unsurprisingly—hungry, oyster-eating humans don't want to look down at their lovely tray of oysters and see a shell covered in mud-filled blisters. Shell-boring polychaetes are not a health risk for people in any way, shape, or form. You could eat one of these worms and you would be fine. But they do ruin the lovely, pearly whiteness of an oyster shell, and by reducing the beauty of this product, they can also reduce its price. Shell-boring polychaetes are therefore the enemy of oyster farmers.

This is a mega bummer. Oyster farming is one of the most environmentally friendly ways to produce food, because while they're hanging in their bags, oysters are feeding by filtering particles out of water—essentially cleaning up the water they're living in. Want to support your local oyster farms? Next time you're eating in a restaurant, order oysters—and if you see blisters or burrows on the oyster shell, just slurp with your eyes closed.

~ 14 ~

ONE GLASS OF DATE PALM SAP, AND HOLD THE BAT PEE

In chapter 11, we discussed a **parasite** (the black death bacterium, *Yersinia pestis*) that ravaged Europe in the Middle Ages. But lest you think that humans have entirely escaped the reach of deadly parasites, I want to tell you now about a modern-day **plague**—one that, like the black death, has a surprising connection to animals.

Imagine that you are growing up in Bangladesh. I've been there, and I'll tell you that it is perhaps the coolest place I have ever visited. Nestled right up against India, Bangladesh is a tropical country of busy cities and lovely rural landscapes—think palm trees, pink sunsets, and, of course, bats. Lots and lots of bats. So many bats that, in the capital city of Dhaka, you can see fruit bats the size of terriers soaring among the tall buildings. But in your mind, I want you to go not to bustling Dhaka but to a small village far from any city: the kind of setting in which most Bangladeshis live. The home you share with your family sits alongside several others, shaded by a grove of tall palm trees. And for breakfast each morning, rather than orange juice, you look forward to a nice tall glass of date palm sap.

What's date palm sap? Well, it is sap of the date palm, a special kind of palm tree that is common in Bangladesh and lots of other tropical countries. You might be familiar with how maple syrup is made, and date palm sap production is very similar. Many trees create sap, which is a sweet, sticky liquid that basically serves as the blood of a tree, carrying nutrients and fluids from one part of the tree to another. To collect this sap, a person will cut a gash into the trunk of a tree, causing the sweet sap within to drip slowly into a bucket waiting below. If you do this to a maple tree, the result is maple syrup, but if you do it to a date palm tree, the result is date palm sap, which is less thick and sweet than maple syrup and isn't put on pancakes but instead makes for a refreshing beverage.

Unfortunately, humans are not the only ani-mals who love date palm sap. Bats also have a sweet tooth. When night throws a blanket of darkness and quiet over your family's village, the village humans might snuggle up and sleep, but the bats are just waking. They've spent the daylight hours hanging upside down from tree branches, swaddled by their own wings. And they're hungry.

The fruit bats that are common in Bangladesh normally eat (as their name would suggest) fruit, but this can be a tough life for a bat. Every sin-gle night, each bat must find a nice ripe mango still hanging from a mango tree, chew through the skin, and then chow down on the mango flesh within. Exhausting! That's why, if they have the option, the bats would much prefer to drink their breakfast. When a bat searching for mangoes instead finds a bucket that humans have hung to collect date palm sap, it has hit the jackpot! It licks the sap as it drips down into the bucket. I know, terrible manners. But it gets worse. Because sometimes, it'll also pee in the date palm sap bucket.

As the sun rises, our lucky bat knows it needs to head home to its roost. It'll reluctantly tear itself away from the date palm sap bucket and head home to dangle from its toes for another day. And later that morning, when your unsuspecting dad comes along to collect that bucket, he won't know that he is pouring bat saliva and pee into a glass for your morning sugar fix.

As if it isn't disgusting and awful enough to accidentally drink bat fluids—it's also dangerous. Bats carry many parasites that can cause **disease** in humans; the rabies virus is one that many of us worry about, but there is a whole universe of other bat-associated viruses that sometimes spill over from bats into people. The COVID-19 pandemic started when a human contracted a bat virus. Same for Ebola. But in your village in Bangladesh, the biggest worry is Nipah virus.

Nipah is a terrible disease. It starts kind of like the flu, with fever, headache, and a sore throat. But, in an unlucky subset of infected

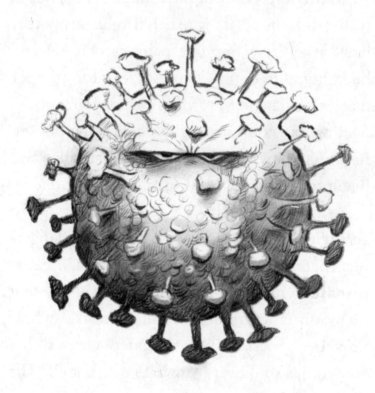

Nipah virus

people, it will later cause the brain to swell, damaging the organ that controls all of your other organs. Some Nipah patients will experience seizures, fall into a coma, and die. In fact, the virus kills about 75 percent of the people it infects (making it one of the world's deadliest viruses), but you're one of the lucky ones. After you recover from your illness, you swear off date palm sap. "Never again!" you tell your dad. But a few weeks later, when that craving for sugar hits, the sparkling glass of date palm sap set on the kitchen table will look tempting . . .

Luckily, Nipah virus isn't common. Only a handful of cases are diagnosed each year, on this planet where billions of people live. But even if you don't favor date palm sap for your morning beverage, the animals that live around you may still put parasites in your path.

~ 15 ~

MAN'S BEST FRIENDS

Dogs are born to love and be loved by humans. I mean this literally. Dogs evolved from wolves, a species that decidedly does not love humans. But many thousands of years ago, some wolves figured out that if they would just be chill and put a pause on all the man-eating, they could hang out near some cave people's fire. If those wolves were super chill, the cave folks would throw them leftovers. And this started a long process of evolution: The cuter, gentler, more loving wolves were favorites of cave people, were fed more, and therefore had more puppies, and to those puppies they passed on their **genes** for cuteness, gentleness, and lovingness. Repeat this for a few thousand generations, and you can begin with a ravening, man-eating wolf, and end up with an adorable, helpless pug. Dogs exist only because humans loved some wolves a long time ago and evolution shaped those wolves into a new species that loves humans back.

But where there is love, there can also be betrayal. Every species on Earth has its own unique set of **parasites** and, any time two species decide to hang out, they risk passing their parasites to each other. This is why your parents won't let you lick your box turtle (salmonella), put your hedgehog on the kitchen table (salmonella again), or get a pet tree squirrel (mpox virus). Just like any other species, dogs have their own unique set of parasites. Close contact between humans and dogs can result in humans becoming accidental **hosts** for some of these dog parasites.

If you live with a dog, you already know about some of the parasites that they can carry.

In many parts of the world, dog owners give monthly heartworm medicine to their beloved pooches; this treatment prevents a pup from becoming infected with worms that like to set up shop inside dog hearts. Dogs all over the world are vaccinated against rabies, a fatal virus that your best bud can contract if they are bitten by an infected mammal like a bat, raccoon, or fox. And most dog owners need to treat their puppers for fleas and ticks using pills or a chemical-treated collar.

But few people know about a worm that is found in dog intestines all over the world. *Dipylidium caninum* (pronounced die-pill-ID-ee-um cay-NINE-um) is, charmingly, also called the cucumber tapeworm. Like any good tapeworm, the cucumber tapeworm looks like a long strand of unspooled tape when it is living as an adult inside its dog host's intestine (remember chapter 9?). That long strand of adult tapeworm is made up of many hundreds of segments, each of which contains both male and female reproductive parts. Once a segment has mated and is full of fertilized **eggs**, it breaks off from the rest of the adult tapeworm and is passed out into the environment in dog poop. This is where the cucumber tapeworm gets its name: Each of those segments is about the size and shape of a cucumber seed. When dog owners reach down to scoop a poop with cucumber tapeworm segments in it, they might think: "Where in the world did Toby get a cucumber?"

There is one surefire way to tell the difference between cucumber seeds and tapeworm segments in your dog's poop: Cucumber seeds don't move. That's right. Each cucumber tapeworm segment can squirm around, and not slowly. In fact, sometimes they are not content to wait for your dog to have a bowel movement and instead take some initiative; they wriggle down your dog's intestine, out through its butthole, and into its fur. This gets the cucumber tapeworm to exactly the place it needs to be: dog fur, where it is possible that it will be eaten up by a larval dog flea. Fleas serve as the tapeworm's **intermediate host**, and the worm's larval stage lives happily in the larval flea until the flea grows up into an adult and the inevitable happens: Your pup gets itchy from flea bites and starts nibbling her skin to scratch that itch. If she swallows an infected flea in the process, the larval tapeworm will sense the stomach acid of the pup, bust out of the flea, and transform into a long, lovely adult tapeworm with lots of segments all its own, completing the life cycle.

It's gross enough to find crawling cucumber tapeworm segments in your dog's poop. Now imagine that you finish your business, peer into the toilet bowl, and see those segments in your own . . . deposit. Humans can become infected with cucumber tapeworms, and those long, segmented adults live happily in the human intestine and shed segments into human feces. If they get impatient, they might even crawl out your butt! While this is probably pretty disturbing, the worms don't pose much of a danger to people and can be easily treated with drugs prescribed by a doctor.

How do humans become infected with cucumber tapeworms? Ironically, it's love that does us in. Most people who become infected

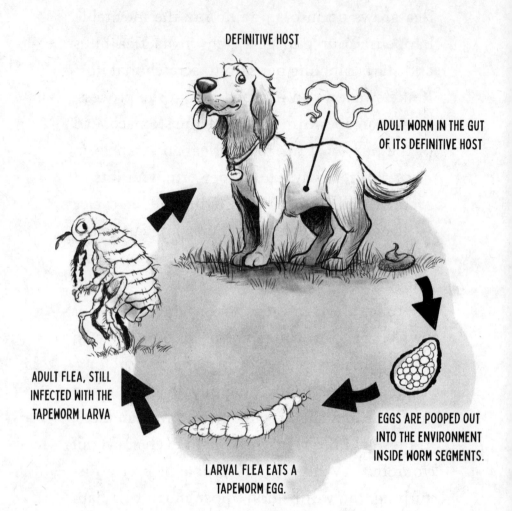

DEFINITIVE HOST

ADULT WORM IN THE GUT
OF ITS DEFINITIVE HOST

EGGS ARE POOPED OUT
INTO THE ENVIRONMENT
INSIDE WORM SEGMENTS.

LARVAL FLEA EATS A
TAPEWORM EGG.

ADULT FLEA, STILL
INFECTED WITH THE
TAPEWORM LARVA

Life cycle of Dipylidium caninum

are kids who really love their dogs. That is, the more you nuzzle and kiss your pup, the greater the likelihood that you will accidentally swallow an infected flea hanging out in your dog's fur. Once that tiny flea is in your intestine, the cucumber tapeworm knows exactly what to do. This horrifying outcome is easily prevented. If you notice cucumber worm segments in your dog's poop, just take her to the vet, who will prescribe a special medicine to kill the worms. You should also make sure that your pet is given regular preventive treatment for fleas. And it never hurts to wash your hands after you give your dog a pat.

I bet the cat people reading this are feeling pretty smug right now. But just because you love cats instead of dogs doesn't mean that you are safe from the reach of pet parasites.

16

BEWARE OF CAT

As we saw in the case of the cucumber tapeworm, bringing pets into the house means bringing two species—dogs and humans, for example— into close quarters. And whenever two species are close enough to share the same couch, they will share their **parasites**. Cats are no exception. In fact, cats host one of the wiliest, smartest, most successful parasites in the entire world. And when you invite a cat into your home, you invite that sneaky parasite in as well.

Toxoplasma gondii (pronounced TALK-zo-plaz-muh GONE-dee-eye) is a tiny, single-celled parasite that I like to call "toxo" for short. But whatever you call it, toxo lives in the intestine of cats, where it mates and produces **eggs**. Those eggs are (you guessed it) shed into the environment in the cat's poop. In fact, when a cat first becomes infected, each number two he produces can contain millions of these eggs! Eggs remain infectious for many months, which gives plenty of time for the turd in which they were originally embedded to be decomposed into soil and for the eggs within to be scattered far and wide. (Turds can be directly deposited in the outdoors by cats, or they may come from improper kitty litter disposal, like dumping litter outside or putting it in a compost pile.) From there, the eggs can contaminate grass, vegetables growing in a garden or field, garbage—anything. Rodents like rats and mice become **hosts** to the larval stages of the parasite (called **cysts**) if they accidentally eat toxo eggs while feeding.

Now, here's where things get weird. Toxo can just hang out in the rodent host and wait for that rodent to get eaten by a cat. If that

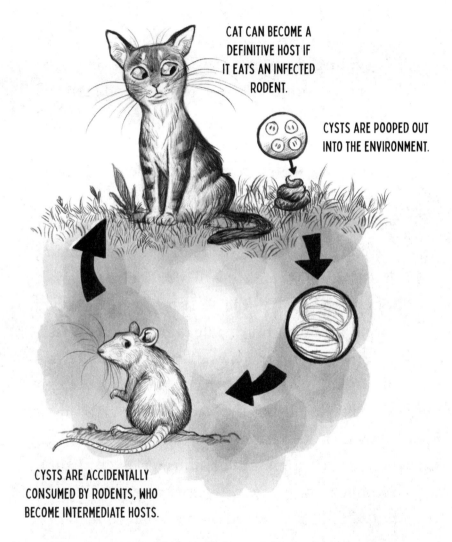

Life cycle of Toxoplasma gondii

happens, then woooo-hoooo for toxo! Winding up in the gut of a cat is its mission in life! But if left to their own devices, most rodents will aim to avoid getting eaten by a cat, so toxo does something pretty tricky: It turns its rodent hosts from timid to dangerously reckless. Uninfected rodents are terrified of the smell of cat pee because it usually means that there is a danger-ous predator nearby. When uninfected rodents smell cat pee, they run away from it, hide, and are extra vigilant to ensure that the pee-er can't sneak up on them. Infected rodents, however, loooooooooooove the stench of cat pee. They love it so much, they run toward it—and possi-bly straight into the jaws of a cat. By manipulat-ing its rodent host's behaviors, toxo increases the likelihood that the host will be eaten by a cat, which is exactly what toxo wants.

Toxo is common in house cats. By some estimates, one out of every three cats in US households is infected with toxo at some point in its life. Infections are found mainly in cats that are allowed to go outside. This is because your beloved Fluffy cannot become infected from kibble or other packaged food; he needs to hunt rodents in order to ingest toxo **cysts**. If your indoor cat catches a mouse in the house or you feed him raw meat, he may develop toxo, but it's primarily outdoor cats that carry infections. If your cat does become infected, you (and your cat) will probably never know. Unlike the infected rodents, infected cats usually show no symptoms. A particularly unlucky cat may become lethargic and feverish, but toxo only rarely causes cats to become sick.

Okay, this parasite doesn't seem like it's a big deal for cats—so why should you care about it? Well, we humans like to believe that we are the most complex **organisms** on Earth, that we can easily outsmart any other species. While I grant that humans are pretty sharp, there are a number of considerably less sophisticated organisms that can nonetheless outwit us. Toxo is one of them.

Humans can become infected with toxo in two ways: by accidentally eating eggs from cat poop or by eating cysts from the muscle of an infected host. First things first: cat poop.

If you clean a kitty litter box and fail to wash your hands afterward or if you allow your cat to pad around on your kitchen counters, eggs from cat feces can be transferred onto your food or directly into your mouth. (This can also happen if you accidentally eat eggs deposited by cats outdoors. Sandboxes are a favorite place for outdoor cats to poop—they are basically large, outdoor litter boxes. As you already know, eggs remain infectious for many months—long after the telltale turd has disappeared!) Alternately, you may accidentally consume cysts in the muscle of an infected host. Usually, people do not become infected by eating rats. Some folks eat rats—don't yuck someone else's yum!—but it isn't all that common. Luckily for toxo, lots of other species can develop muscle cysts from eating toxo eggs, including pigs, sheep, and cows, which pick up their infections while grazing on grass that has been pooped on by a cat. Thoroughly cooking meat kills the toxo cysts, but if you like your hamburgers rare, there is a chance that you will consume a living toxo cyst and become infected yourself. That's when the fun begins.

Toxo doesn't gain anything from manipulating the behavior of a human, because humans rarely get eaten by cats. That is, humans are a dead-end host for toxo, because the parasite will never be transferred from a human host into its desired cat host (barring some extremely grim scenarios). But that doesn't stop toxo from trying. In terms of how our bodies work, humans are actually pretty similar to rats, so much so that toxo can pull the same levers in a human host that it pulls in a rat host and wind up with roughly the same result. Infected humans have slower reaction times than uninfected humans, and as a result are about three times as likely to get into car accidents. Remember that rodents infected with toxo are risk-takers, becoming attracted to the smell of their mortal enemy, the cat? Well, there is some evidence to suggest that infected humans are more likely to pursue risky careers, where the likelihood of failure is high—like starting your own business. But things get even kookier, because some of the effects of toxo on your behavior appear to depend on your sex. Infected men are more likely to disregard rules than are uninfected men, and also tend to be more suspicious and jealous. Infected women are more likely to follow rules than are uninfected women, and also tend to be more warmhearted and outgoing. No one knows why toxo infection has these divergent effects on men versus women, but it certainly makes me wonder about some of the people in my life.

Toxo has definitely earned the title of "world's most successful parasite": Around the globe, approximately one out of every three people has been infected with toxo. But that rate varies depending on where you are in the world—in some places, it is higher, and in other places, lower. In the United States, only about one in ten humans has been infected, because the country has a temperate climate (cold isn't good for toxo cysts) and good sanitation (the US system for managing cat poop and other waste is pretty effective). Those are better odds, but still: If you are an American who knows ten people, you probably know at least one person who is harboring toxo cysts in their own body. Now think about your family

We like to think that we have free will. But are
we actually puppets being controlled by our
parasite puppet masters?

members, friends, schoolmates, teachers . . . any risk-takers? Maybe you know someone who is particularly prone to accidents? Knowing that toxo is out there, hidden from sight but pulling the strings like a puppet master behind a curtain, maybe you'll rethink your uncle who doesn't trust the government or your warm, loving grandmother who talks your ear off.

See what I mean about learning **parasitology**? It's like getting a chance to peer into an alternate dimension. Beneath his fluffy surface, your cat contains an entire world that was previously hidden from you. But your cat isn't the only one, because there is also plenty going on beneath *your* surface.

17

A SPOONFUL OF SUGAR HELPS THE PARASITES GO DOWN

Picture in your mind a healthy person. You probably imagine strong muscles, boundless energy, and definitely no **parasites** tucked away in this person's innards. We usually think of parasites as a cause of poor health—after all, people who wind up with parasitic infections can suffer from a range of awful symptoms, including pain, exhaustion, and even death. A healthy person could never be **host** to a mass of writhing worms . . . could they?

As it turns out, a few worms in your intestine might not be as bad as you'd think. New scientific research is changing our perceptions of what a "healthy" human looks like. Consider this: Over the past several decades, there has been a tidal wave of **autoimmune diseases**, like seasonal allergies, asthma, Crohn's disease, ulcerative colitis, lupus, and multiple sclerosis. Perhaps you know (or are) a person with one of these diseases—and if so, you are not alone. For example, from 2013 to 2020 (just eight years!), the number of people with multiple sclerosis increased by 50 percent to 2.8 million.

On the surface, these autoimmune diseases seem to have little in common with one another. After all, Crohn's disease causes diarrhea while multiple sclerosis causes the **nervous system** to degenerate—the symptoms couldn't be more different. But the source of the symptoms is the same. In all autoimmune diseases, the **immune system** turns on itself and begins attacking the body's own organs. Under normal circumstances, the immune system is meant to keep out foreign invaders. When you cut your skin, the immune system sends **cells** to kill any **bacteria** introduced into the bloodstream before they can multiply; when a parasite enters your gut, the immune system sends cells to terminate that parasite before it can set up shop. But for people with autoimmune diseases, all the firepower of the immune system turns inward, and the results can range from uncomfortable to deadly.

No one knows why autoimmune diseases are so much more common than they used to be. But we do have some clues. For one, the increase in autoimmune diseases is happening only in wealthy areas in North America, Europe, and Australia. In the Global South (lower-income countries located mostly in the tropics), autoimmune diseases are almost unheard of. Another clue is that the rise of autoimmune diseases has been happening just as folks in wealthy countries have achieved their long-standing goal of becoming parasite-free. There are many, many parasites of humans, transmitted in a variety of ways. As we have sealed our homes against the elements, started to spend more time indoors than out, made food handling and processing more hygienic, and gotten obsessed with sparkling-clean surfaces, we have won the war against parasites. Most people living in wealthy countries have no worms in their guts. But by leaving behind our worms, we might have made ourselves vulnerable to something much worse.

Scientists suspect that people who have no exposure to parasites in early childhood—like most folks living in the hyper-hygienic wealthy countries—may be more likely to develop autoimmune diseases later in life. The theory is this: Humans evolved alongside their parasites. Our bodies just assume parasites will be there, because for so much of our history, parasites *were* always there. Because our bodies assume that they will fight constant battles with parasites, our immune systems are always spoiling for that fight. Without any parasites to punch, the assault is turned on the body's own organ systems. It's also possible that the parasites themselves might be able to turn down the volume on the immune system's assault; this is an adaptation that the parasites might use to reduce the damage the immune system can do to the worms. But without the parasites there to dial the immunity knob from eleven to two, it stays at eleven—and the body's own organs pay the price.

I know what you're thinking right now. "Wait a second... if a lack of parasites causes auto-immune diseases, can these diseases be cured by infecting a patient with parasites?" The terrifying answer is: maybe! Scientists are still doing experiments and making measurements to determine whether parasitic worms can be used as medicine. But the information we have so far is promising. A clinical trial has shown that doctors can reduce symptoms in multiple sclerosis patients by infecting them with pig whipworm—an intestinal worm usually found in pigs but which also lives quite happily in the human gut. Another clinical trial has helped ulcerative colitis and Crohn's disease patients with the same kind of worm. Yes, parasites are bad for their hosts (by definition). A whipworm is going to do its whipworm thing, chewing on the lining of the intestine and sucking blood. But that might be a small price to pay if, while it is chewing, that worm is also reducing the awful symptoms of multiple sclerosis in its human host.

Please do not take this as license to go out and get yourself a parasite. Parasites can be quite dangerous (as you've read in the many chapters preceding this one). But we are also learning something new about parasites: We can't live with them, but maybe we also can't live without them.

PARTING THOUGHTS

~ 18 ~

POWER TO THE PARASITES!

Sometimes I like to imagine how my life might have turned out if I had made different choices. What if I'd never learned about **parasites** and had instead worked with dolphins and whales like I'd planned when I was a kid? I'm sure that things would have turned out fine—whales and dolphins are interesting enough. But I'm also sure that dolphin-researcher Chelsea would have felt a void, like something was missing. Whales and dolphins are just a few dozen species; parasites are tens of thousands of species, probably a lot more. With whales and dolphins, what you see is what you get; parasites are hidden away, mysterious and shrouded in secrecy. Whales and dolphins are important enough in the marine **ecosystems** where they occur; parasites occur in every eco-system, and wherever they occur they are large and in charge, puppet masters pulling the strings. Being a **parasitologist** is like discovering a secret room in your house—a room that no one else knows about, that is full of treasures, and that only you can access. I can't imagine a life in which I wander around the house, unaware of the secret treasure room right under my nose.

I've now taken you by the hand, walked you to the door of the secret treasure room, showed you some of the treasures contained within, and handed you your very own key so that you can come back whenever you want. What will you do with that key? Now that you know that there are parasites in every animal in every ecosystem, causing moose to flee from deer (chapter 4), fish to swim in circles (chapter 5), birds to boom and bust (chapter 8), and crickets to die by suicide (chapter 10), will you ever be able to look at those animals the same way again? Will you be able to watch your cat walk across the kitchen counter (chapter 16) or nuzzle your puppy (chapter 15) without worry? Will you be an intolerable dinner companion when sushi (chapter 12), oysters (chapter 13), or hamburgers (chapter 16) are served? Will you recommend a dose of parasites when your friend starts her springtime sneezing routine (chapter 17)? When you think of the Middle Ages (chapter 11) or the Mesozoic (chapter 9), will you think of parasites? Will you worry for their fate (chapter 6)?

I hope that this book has proved to you that parasites are many things simultaneously: weird of course, but also important to the health of their ecosystems and beautiful to boot. Maybe you've fallen in love with parasites, or maybe you haven't. But, whatever your opinion of these beasts, I know that from here on out you'll move through the world thinking not just about the life that you can see, but also about the secret world of parasites that lies beneath. I know that when you cross paths with them in the future, you won't recoil, but you'll instead proclaim, "Power to the parasites!"

GLOSSARY

adult parasite—In a complex life cycle, parasites pass through multiple life stages that look very different from one another. The adult stage is the stage of the parasite life cycle in which the parasite undergoes sexual reproduction.

ammonite—A kind of marine invertebrate that went extinct at the end of the Cretaceous period, along with the dinosaurs. Ammonites are closely related to modern-day octopus and squid.

autoimmune disease—Occurs when a person's immune system attacks their own body; for example, seasonal allergies, asthma, Crohn's disease, ulcerative colitis, lupus, and multiple sclerosis.

bacteria—A kind of tiny, microscopic organism that can be found everywhere; some bacteria are parasites (that is, they live in or on a host and cause harm to that host), but others are beneficial (for example, the bacteria that live in your gut and help you digest food), and yet others are free-living (for example, bacteria in soil).

bivalves—A kind of aquatic animal whose body is enclosed in a hinged shell; for example, clams, mussels, and oysters.

cell—A tiny structure that makes up the tissues of all living organisms.

complex life cycle—A kind of parasite life cycle in which the parasite requires at least two different host species to complete its development. The parasite passes through multiple life stages in the process of moving from one host species to the next. These life stages can look very different from one another. Any life stage that undergoes sexual reproduction is considered an adult parasite, and any stage that undergoes asexual reproduction or no reproduction is considered a larval parasite.

crustacean—A kind of animal with jointed appendages; for example, crabs, lobsters, shrimp, and some kinds of plankton.

cyst—The "waiting stage" of a parasite, in which a larval parasite wraps itself up in a protective cocoon until it reaches its next host.

definitive host—In a complex life cycle, the host in which sexual reproduction takes place.

disease—Any condition in which the normal functioning of the body is impaired; for example, the coronavirus parasite causes the disease COVID-19.

ecosystem—A geographic area where organisms of many species occur together; for example, a coral reef is an ecosystem, a forest is an ecosystem, and a meadow is an ecosystem.

eggs—Just like chickens, many parasites produce eggs, from which their babies hatch.

first intermediate host—In a complex life cycle, the host of the first larval stage of a parasite.

fossil—Fossils are formed when the body of a prehistoric organism is preserved in rock.

free-living—A term used to describe any organism that does not live inside or on a host.

gene—The material that is inherited by offspring from their parents, which determines the offspring's characteristics. For example, you might inherit your parents' genes for black hair or for being very tall.

grub—The larva of an insect.

host—Any organism that is the victim of a parasite.

immune system—The cells, tissues, and organs of the body that are responsible for fighting off foreign organisms or substances, including parasites.

intermediate host—In a complex life cycle, the host of any larval stage of a parasite. Note that first intermediate hosts are hosts of the first larval stage of a parasite, and second intermediate hosts are hosts of the second larval stage.

krill—Tiny crustaceans that live in the ocean, usually as plankton.

larvae—(singular: **larva**; adjective: **larval**) Juvenile stages of a parasite; essentially, baby parasites. Larval parasites don't undergo sexual reproduction but can undergo asexual reproduction.

malaria—A disease caused by single-celled *Plasmodium* parasites.

nervous system—The cells, tissues, and organs that are responsible for sensing the outside world and responding to it.

neurological—Relating to the nervous system, which controls thoughts, feelings, and behaviors.

organism—A living thing.

parasite—Any organism that lives inside or on a host and causes harm to that host.

parasitoid—A parasitoid is a special kind of parasite that uses its host's body for a period of time before ultimately killing the host. While most parasites want to keep their host alive so that they can continue to exploit it, parasitoids need their host to die in order to move on to the next stage in their life cycle.

parasitologist—A scientist who studies parasites.

parasitology—The scientific study of parasites.

plague—Any infectious disease event that causes a lot of death and destruction. For example, COVID-19 has been described as a plague. However, when people say "*the* plague," they are usually referring to the black death, a massive infectious disease event caused by the bacterium *Yersinia pestis*. You can read more about the plague in chapter 11.

plankton—A kind of tiny, usually microscopic organism that lives in ocean waters and drifts with the ocean currents.

second intermediate host—In a complex life cycle, the host of the second larval stage of a parasite.

vertebrate—An animal with a backbone. For example, humans, dogs, birds, frogs, snakes, and fish are all vertebrates; insects, snails, clams, and most parasites are not vertebrates and are therefore called invertebrates.

wingspan—In birds, the distance from one wing tip to the other when the wings are outstretched.

ACKNOWLEDGMENTS

This work has been vetted and improved by many scientists and science communicators. My thanks to the subject-matter experts who provided scientific reviews of the chapters pertaining to their expertise, including Jerri Bartholomew, Julia Buck, Rob Dunn, Skylar Hopkins, Mike Hsieh, Armand Kuris, Kevin Lafferty, Arne Levsen, Chenhua Li, Tim Littlewood, Steve Luby, Dana Morse, Paul Rawson, Dan Salkeld, Sam Silverbrand, Susanne Sokolow, Kelly Weinersmith, and Tiffany Wolf. I'm indebted to members of my lab at the University of Washington who provided commentary on early versions of some chapters, including Danielle Claar, Sara Faiad, Aspen Katla, Katie Leslie, Julieta Martinelli, Natalie Mastick, Emily Oven, Whitney Preisser, Rachel Welicky, and Maureen Williams. Peg Herring offered excellent advice on writing for a middle grade audience.

An equal amount of useful feedback on drafts of this manuscript came from kid reviewers. Big thanks to the following young readers and their families: Wesley Armstrong, Robert Galin, Wyatt Hostetter, Owen Kelly, Dylan Liamero, Miles Taylor, Cecilia Valero, Jasper Ward, Ada Weinersmith, and Hannah Yamashita. And more big thanks to Emily McFadden and her seventh-grade classes at I.S. 126: Albert Shanker School for Visual and Performing Arts in Queens, New York.

This book would not exist if Laura Godwin at Godwin Books had not heard me gushing about parasites on NPR. Thank you, Laura, for envisioning a children's book on such slimy, scary, yucky subject matter. Rachel Murray and Kortney Nash helped shepherd the manuscript at Godwin Books. My agent, Renee Zuckerbrot, was an endlessly patient educator and guide for this first-time author.

Just as I am inducting you into the world of parasitology, I was inducted long ago by some extremely generous, patient, and brilliant scientists. Jeb Byers and Kathy Cottingham gave me my first job as a parasite ecologist. Armand Kuris, Kevin Lafferty, and Ryan Hechinger provided my formal training in parasite ecology. And my PhD adviser, Fio Micheli, and post-doc adviser, Piet Johnson, gave me the freedom and support I needed to learn and grow as a parasite ecologist. I wouldn't be living the life parasitic without them.

Finally, thanks to the fortitudinous folks who have endured many tales of poop and worms at the dinner table: Ken Ferguson, Virginia Linn, Emily Wood, Bobby Wood, Alison Haupt, Ana Sofía Guerra, and Sarah Lee. You are the test pilots for all my parasite stories.